TECHNOLOGY USE IN OPEN LEARNING SYSTEM

TECHNOLOGY USE IN OPEN LEARNING SYSTEM

Editor
Prof. Ramesh Chandra

Publications
KALPAZ PUBLICATIONS
DELHI-110052

TECHNOLOGY USE IN OPEN LEARNING SYSTEM

Technology Use in Open Learning System

Rs. 880

ISBN: 81-7835-235-4

This book is Vol. No. 7 of Universal Education and Technology in 21st Century (Set)

Published in 2005 in India by
Kalpaz Publications,
C-30, Satyawati Nagar, Delhi-110052
E-mail : Kalpaz@hotmail.com

Laser Typesetting at : Master Computers, Delhi
Printed at : Ajit Printers, Delhi

Contents

Preface

We are facing a time of information evolution. In the ever-changing world filled with new technology, our teachers and students require the right information, from the right sources, today. Educational technology is looming as a preeminent force in open learning system. The development of interactive multimedia learning environments has allowed to teach things that were found difficult to teach. Educational technology has fostered the advancement of active-learning pedagogies in teaching. It has improved the ability to exploit new insights about the cognitive development of learning. The utility of the computer to monitor student progress has encouraged to think more carefully about assessment and to strive for the development of assessment tools that allow to give students more individual attention.

For education professionals computer networking creates a professional bond between teachers and administrators, ends isolation. For students a new system of knowledge will enhance collaborative learning; alternative assessment; and individualised learning. Rather than debating the connections between technology-based instruction and test scores, schools should focus on the most obvious and compelling reason form implementing technology-namely, that students need strong technology skills to succeed in the world of work.

This book provides a comprehensive analysis on technology use in the open learning system. It provides an authentic account of elements and processes that need to be considered in the context of increasing access to information and communication technologies, at all levels of education. Teachers, trainers, policy makers, researchers, curriculum developers, multimedia software engineers and educational equipment manufactures will find it indispensable.

Editor

Chapter 1

Dimensions of Distance Education

Although distance education is far from new, having roots extending to nineteenth-century correspondence courses, digital technologies have fostered a rapid expansion in recent years, as well as a change in profile. Many more distance education courses are being offered than ever before, and the number is growing exponentially. The technologies used in distance education, the populations served, the institutions offering distance education programs, and the partnerships that have emerged among providers differ in nature and scale from earlier models.

Distance education is utilized at every level of the educational spectrum. It takes different forms, however, at different levels. The most extensive use as a substitute for the classroom experience is in higher education.

Elementary and secondary school students are using computers in increasing numbers. According to the US Department of Education, 89% of public schools had access to the Internet as of the fall of 1998, as did 51% of individual classrooms. Computer use in elementary and secondary education, however, does not generally involve distance education in the sense described above, in which the course as a whole is delivered remotely. Rather, education in this area tends to focus on software packages designed to be used as an adjunct to classroom instruction. These could include computer programs in basic reading or math that the student can use at home, or in-class projects that involve using computers as research or learning aids.

At the higher levels of secondary education, distance education activities are more extensive. Distance education programs are providing high-school students with the opportunity to take classes not otherwise available to them, such as advanced placement or college equivalency courses, through remote means. In addition, there is at least one project underway to create a complete accredited high school diploma sequence available through the Internet.

The field of post-secondary distance education is growing most rapidly. Courses are available in community colleges and universities, at the post-graduate level, for professional development and training, and for continuing education. Community colleges, with their history of serving local and continuing education communities, have been particularly active, as have many university systems.

Today's distance education courses use digital technology extensively for varied purposes and in varied ways. The addition of digital technologies to the distance education palette has produced new models of learning, resulting in a richer and more interactive class environment.

Evolution of distance education technologies. Radio was a favored medium for distance education in the first part of the twentieth century, with television supplanting it in the 1950s. Telecourses produced by educators and distributed by the Public Broadcasting Service ("PBS"), for example, have had a large audience since the 1950s. Such telecourses and video are still widely used, and are expanding their services in both the analog and digital environment.

The 1990s have seen the advent of computer networks and multimedia technologies as a powerful new addition to the tools of distance education. These last several years. According to a study done by the U.S. Department of Education, in 1995, over 70% of higher education institutions were planning to start or increase offering courses using online or other computer-based technologies in the next three years.

Currently, distance education programs use combinations of available technologies in varied ways. These may involve one or more of the following: e-mail among teachers and students, class chat rooms, links to resources on the World Wide Web, incorporation of preexisting content in the course of instruction, and the delivery of supplementary materials in electronic form. The use of older technologies, like videoconferencing, is also prevalent, particularly by rural schools.

Even in distance education courses delivered entirely through digital media, however, students continue to use textbooks. The determination of which technologies are to be used in a distance education course is generally based on the intended audience for the course, and the availability and cost of the technology. Older working students, for example, may require fewer multimedia "bells and whistles" than the average college student, and programs prepared for them may focus more on unvarnished text. Rural students or students in other countries may have less access to sophisticated equipment with advanced capabilities.

One of the most significant ways in which distance education has evolved is its shift from one-way technologies to interactive technologies. Many educators try to incorporate interactive elements into their distance education classes, but in the past they were limited by the technologies available to them. The traditional model for distance education has been the one-way transmission of instruction from teacher to remote students, with interaction between the instructor and the student, or between the students themselves, often limited to phone lines or correspondence.

The addition of digital technologies enables more teacher-to-student and student-to-student interaction. E-mail and chat rooms, for example, allow continuous collegial discourse among students separated by distance. As a result of the new technologies, distance education programs are offering a more interactive experience that more closely parallels face-to-face teaching-in effect creating a virtual classroom.

The new technologies have also made distance education courses more convenient and better suited to the needs of different students. Historically, distance education programs have been divided into two categories, synchronous and asynchronous. Examples of the former are programs delivered by broadcast and closed circuit technologies, which are set in real time, allowing the student to participate from a distance, but imposing scheduling constraints.

Traditional asynchronous programs are exemplified by correspondence and videotape courses. They allow for a time lapse between the delivery of material by an instructor and its reception by a student, but do not involve "live" elements.

With the advent of interoperable digital media, distance education has increasingly incorporated both synchronous and asynchronous tools into the same course, providing students with the benefits of both.

Asynchronous technologies, such as e-mail, threaded discussion and self-paced testing, are often used in conjunction with synchronous elements such as chat rooms and streaming audio. The same material may be delivered by botsynchronous and asynchronous methods. For example, a lecture may be delivered in real time by streaming audio, and then archived and made available to students for later review.

In the course of providing distance education programs, institutions draw on their library resources in several ways. Often, they rely on librarians in negotiating and obtaining licenses, since librarians tend to have experience in this area. Libraries also provide facilities and support staff for making online courses available to students, assist in preparing materials in digital form, and advise on copyright law.

Frequently, distance educators provide access to selected library resources in digital form for their classes. These selected resources may be designated as electronic reserves, or "e-reserves," similar in concept to the use of reserve materials for on-campus classes, which the instructor sets aside for outside reading to supplement primary course materials. These or other electronic resource materials are sometimes made available to remote-site students pursuant to institutional licenses obtained through the library.

Educational institutions are making significant efforts to adopt and implement appropriate policies on the copyright issues involved in distance education. These efforts include promulgating written policies, conducting training for faculty and staff, and educating students about copyright law.

As distance education programs become increasingly incorporated into mainstream curricula, the issue of accreditation has become a focus of attention. Essential to the continued success of distance education courses is public acceptance of such courses as comparable in quality to classroom instruction. This is an important issue both for students, who must choose among available programs, and for educators who must assess the knowledge imparted. by those programs. Formal accreditation has traditionally provided that assurance of quality.

Many distance education programs offered by nonprofit public and private universities are formally accredited by the same bodies that provide accreditation to those institutions for traditional courses and programs. For-profit universities have also recently begun to receive accreditation by these bodies. Some have raised questions about the standards for accreditation in this context, on the ground that distance education courses have unique characteristics that require specialized evaluation.

Regional accrediting bodies, for example, will have to find new ways to evaluate distance education programs with dispersed components such as administrative offices located far from academic headquarters. In addition, some distance education programs may involve stand-alone courses offered through collaboration among multiple institutions, rather than by a single already-accredited institution. This can pose problems for bodies that have traditionally accredited only institutions as a whole.

Distance education helps students overcome such barriers as full-time work commitments, geographic inaccessibility, the difficulty of obtaining child or elder care, and physical disabilities. It can also provide the advantage of convenience and flexibility. With digital technologies enabling courses to reach and appeal to wider audiences, interest in distance education is growing. It has been predicted that by 2002, the number of students taking distance courses will represent 15% of all higher education students, up from 5% in 1998.

While all segments of the population are reached by the range of courses offered today, the college audience is increasing at a particularly rapid pace. According to recent statistics, the number of college students enrolled in distance learning courses will reach 2.2 million in 2002, up from 710,000 in 1998.

Distance education owes much of its explosive growth over the last decades to its responsiveness to the needs of an older, non-traditional student population. The average distance education student is thirty-four, employed full-time and has previous college experience. More than half are female. Students in other countries are also increasingly served by U.S. digital distance education programs, allowing them to benefit from educational opportunities without relocating.

Many students drawn to distance education at higher education levels are professionals whose jobs prevent them from attending classes on a campus. This is a fact that institutions offering distance education courses have recognized. Even traditional private universities like Harvard, Stanford and Duke, known for their on-campus degree programs, are developing distance courses for working adults. Such courses are often geared towards professional development or training.

Retirees often take advantage of distance education opportunities as well. Greater disposable income and/or greater leisure may lead older students to take courses for life-enhancing reasons, rather than for academic or professional advancement. Senior citizens may choose to take courses online due to restricted mobility or a desire to study privately. The expansion of the field of distance education has led to changes among its providers. Although many distance education programs are offered by established public and private colleges and universities, the traditional model of nonprofit K-12 and post-secondary nonprofit and for-profit entities, on both a nonprofit and for-profit basis, and through varieties of partnerships involving both educational institutions and corporations.

Providers of distance education courses and components of courses cover a broad spectrum. There are providers at the K-12 level, among community colleges, among public and private universities, in continuing education, and among educational publishers. There are also providers who are solely engaged in the provision of distance education courses, sometimes called "virtual" universities.

With greater technological capabilities available and increasing technological sophistication among educators, the number of institutions offering digital distance education has correspondingly increased. It has been predicted that by 2002, 85% of two-year colleges will be offering distance learning courses, up from 58% in 1998, and 84% of four-year colleges will be offering distance learning courses, up from 62% in 1998.

A number of well-known schools are already offering entire degree programs online, such as Stanford University, the University of Illinois and Western Governors University. Consortia have been formed to pool resources and offer classes from multiple institutions. For example, the Colorado Community College Online offers 35 courses from 12 different accredited institutions. The Southern Regional Electronic Campus carries approximately 1,500 credit courses and 60 degree programs from 175 different colleges. Western Governors University offers courses from over 30 institutions across the United States.

In the United States, academic and professional education has become a $100 billion a year business. This fact, combined with the increasing public appetite for distance education courses, is having an effect on the roles played by providers. Once a primarily nonprofit activity, distance education is now perceived as a potentially lucrative market. Nonprofit institutions continue to offer nonprofit courses, but new for-profit educational institutions have entered the field, while some nonprofit institutions have begun to engage in distance education activities for profit.

The predominant model remains nonprofit. Schools at all levels continue to produce distance education offerings on a nonprofit basis. The tuition paid for a distance education course at these institutions is typically no different than that charged for an on-campus course, although additional fees may be charged to cover technology costs. For-profit entities play an increasing role in distance education.

There are a number of educational institutions, with the University of Phoenix ("UOP") the most well-known example. As the largest for-profit based university in the country, the UOP online campus enrolls about 9,000 students. Corporate entities, such as commercial publishers, are also entering this market directly as providers of full-service distance education curricula. A hybrid category is comprised of nonprofit educational institutions that are launching for-profit distance education projects.

New York University, for example, is planning to create a wholly-owned, for-profit subsidiary to offer online courses apart from those offered by the university itself. The courses will be marketed to corporations, colleges and universities, and individual students. The subsidiary will enable the university to earn money through a stock offering or the sale of partnership interests.

Two distinct varieties of partnership have emerged as the result of the growth of distance education, one between nonprofit and commercial entities, and the other among educational institutions. In recognition of the value of the educational market, and the need for courses tailored to accommodate busy schedules and business training needs, corporations have partnered with universities to design, produce and transmit distance education courses.

One major benefit of these arrangements is that educational institutions have the costs of expensive distance education technologies defrayed by their corporate partners, while the corporate partners "acquire an invaluable 'laboratory' for application of their technology in educational environments, and often gain access to the latest research of leading academics as reflected in their curriculum." AT&T, for example, has designed a Learning Network Virtual Academy In partnership with a number of colleges and universities, including Pennsylvania State University and the George Washington University, which offers a range of professional development options for educators. Educational publishers are also increasingly collaborating with educators to create courses to be marketed commercially.

Educational institutions, recognizing the potential of sharing resources and expertise in this expanding field, are collaborating with each other to create programs that span state lines and university systems. Colleges and universities have a long history of association, and distance education has provided new incentives to develop partnerships with peer institutions. These partnerships, such as the consortia discussed above, can provide a mechanism for different institutions to offer classes through a unified distribution system, or for institutions new to the field of distance education to access an infrastructure through which to offer online courses. They can also allow institutions to benefit from access to each other's faculty, with two or more institutions sharing faculty and technological support to create a class offered by both institutions.

The federal government has been active in recognizing and promoting the benefits of distance education. This section describes a few key pieces of federal legislation. The Higher Education Amendments Act of 1998 ("HEA") is the most far-reaching and recent federal legislation addressing distance education. Through this legislation, the government provides financial aid for distance education students, authorizes funding for the development of distance education programs, and establishes a high-level "Web-Based Education Commission" to assess the educational software available for students.

(a) *Student financial aid.* The HEA enables selected distance education programs to offer their students funding under federal student grant and loan programs. Distance education students have long been ineligible for many such government benefits. The "50 percent rule" has traditionally excluded institutions offering more than 50% of their courses remotely, or with more than 50% of their student body enrolled in remote courses, from offering financial aid to their students. The Distance Education Demonstration Program will fund up to fifty institutions over a five-year period, allowing a waiver of this rule.

(b) *Learning Anytime Anywhere Partnerships.* The HEA also establishes the Learning Anytime Anywhere Partnerships Program ("LAAP"), intended to promote "post-secondary . . . and career-oriented lifelong learning" through distance education. LAAP is a five-year grant program that will fund partnerships among "higher education, communityorganizations, and other public and private organizations, agencies and organizations." The funds will be used to develop model distance education programs and supporting activities.

(c) *Web-Based Education Commission.* The amendments also provide for the establishment of a Web-Based

> Education Commission, with fourteen members appointed by the President, the Secretary of Education, and the Congressional leadership. The three members appointed by the President are to represent the Internet technology industry, and the three members appointed by the Secretary are to have "expertise in accreditation, establishing statewide curricula, and establishing information technology networks pertaining to education curricula." The mandate of the Commission is to "conduct a thorough study to assess the educational software available in retail markets for secondary and post-secondary students who choose to use such software."

Although the HEA focuses on post-secondary distance education efforts, federal funding is channeled to the K-12 grades as well. The Star Schools Program, funded through the Office of Educational Research and Improvement at the Department of Education, was begun in 1988 as part of the federal government's work to support school reform efforts. The Star Schools Program was originally intended to increase foreign language, mathematics and science course offerings for K-12 students, but over time has expanded its scope. It may be viewed as a forerunner of the LAAP program, and provides similar funding opportunities to technology projects in the K-12 range.

The Star Schools Program provides grants to eligible telecommunications partnerships "to encourage improved instruction in mathematics, science, foreign language, literacy skills, vocational education, and other subjects, and to serve underserved populations through the development, construction, and acquisition of telecommunications facilities, equipment, and instructional programming." Star Schools grants are used "to obtain telecommunications facilities and equipment; develop and acquire instructional programming for students, staff development for teachers and administrators, and educational programming for parents and community members; and to obtain technical assistance for teachers, school personnel, and other educators in the use of the facilities and programming." Since its inception, the Program has been very successful, awarding more than $125 million to telecommunications partnerships, providing services to more than 6,000 schools, and reaching approximately 1,600,000 learners.

Distance Education Technologies

Technology has assumed an increasingly important role in the evolution of distance education. In the past decade, digital technologies have transformed the way distance education is accomplished, as well as affecting its potential impact on markets for copyrighted works. The relevant technologies can be broken down into three major categories:

1) technologies that facilitate licensing;

2) technologies that deliver the content of the course; and

3) technologies that protect the delivered content.

Within the last category, a further distinction can be made between technologies that restrict access, and technologies that restrict or detect uses of works after access has been gained. One area of technology that facilitates licensing is the ability to attach licensing-related information to a work in a digital format. This information can be linked to or embedded in the work, and accessed by the user. In some instances the user will need special software to read information imperceptibly embedded in the work, and in others he can click on an external link to the information. Information so accessed can identify the copyright owner, point the user to the appropriate licensing site, or list licensing terms and conditions.Also useful are online rights and permissions services that can support a range of license and delivery functions, although not all services offer all functions.

Electronic licensing and electronic delivery are separable, independent activities, and either or both can be accomplished by the same online service. Such services can provide central access to a large group of materials, standardized licensing terms that can be customized according to the content provider, and a quick turn-around time for requests. Several different online rights and permissions services are currently in use or development.

The online permissions process itself allows a high degree of specialization. Menus for these online requests can divide users into different categories and subject them to different licensing terms, including grants of permission without a fee. For example, an educational requester could be asked to specify whether the proposed use is for a classroom, seminar, or dissertation.

Users could be asked to identify themselves as nonprofit or for-profit, accredited or non-accredited, or any other characteristics that are significant to the copyright owner. The user could also respond to standard queries on the method of delivery, the size of the class, or the security of the website.

Any information relevant to the decision whether to license and how much to charge can be obtained, and this information can be used to generate an automatic response based on pre-established agreements between the service and the copyright owner, or to query the copyright owner directly for permission. In addition to processing licensing requests, some services may also accept payment for the license and deliver the content to the user digitally. Depending on the particular service, the material could be delivered with whatever technological protections the copyright owner specifies already attached.

As well as enabling licensing and delivery to take place online, technology can also facilitate access to licensors by the direct linking of works in a digital form to rights and permissions databases. This may be done with a link, such as an icon, at the end of text or an image, that a user may click on to go straight to an online licensing database.

An important development in licensing for digital uses is the convergence of permissions systems with other systems designed to identify and protect material. In the analog world, licensing tends to be a discrete transaction, separate from how the user gains. Access to the material or what the user is able to do with the material once she has it. In the digital world, these functions are converging. A single online site may authorize use of a work, accept payment for that use, deliver a copy of the work to the user, and attach technological protections.

Distance education today is delivered via both analog and digital technologies, including diverse combinations of telephone connections, telecourses, video conferences and computer transmissions. Because our mandate is to consider issues relating to the use of digital technologies, particularly the need for an exemption "for distance education through digital networks," we focus here on the use of digital network technology. Other types of digital technologies may also be used to deliver distance education, such as digital television broadcasts or videoçonferencing. These are examples of traditional media being used to carry digital, instead of analog, information.

Telecourses and video conferences incorporate different degrees of interactivity, and may involve one-way video with two-way audio, or two-way video and two-way audio. At the highest level of interactivity, videoconferencing allows instructors and students to see and speak to each other in real time as if they were in a classroom together. These types of digital technologies function much like their analog counterparts, but are usually capable of carrying more information more efficiently.

It is important to note that even non-networked transmissions, whether digital or analog, may incorporate elements of digital network technology. For example, telecourses or video conferences are often transmitted in conjunction with a computer connection between the students and the instructor, allowing simultaneous online interaction.

The computer is the most versatile of distance education instruments, since it can incorporate or perform the same function as a television or telephone, as well as providing more interactivity, delivering more content, and supporting more comprehensive services than any other single medium. Computers can be used to transmit texts and graphics, connect users in a variety of real-time and asynchronous dialogues, deliver messages between users, and receive both audio and video transmissions.

There are several commercial software products available to help educators construct online courses for students to access through personal computers. These products are basically a template of a blank course website, offering a choice of many of the technologies common to such courses. The instructor is then free to fill in the site with content, and to choose which of the available options she wants to incorporate.

Despite the use of these common templates, there is no "typical" online distance education course. When the concept of a class is transported to a virtual context, it is no longer constrained by the attributes of a physical classroom, such as the duration of a lesson, the ways in which materials can be used in class, and the schedule of the teacher and students.

The virtual classroom can be defined by its ability to be tailored to the needs of different instructors, students and subject matters. The commercial templates are designed to be customized by each instructor. In addition, many instructors, or the information services of their institutions, build their own courses from scratch.

Factors such as the technological sophistication of the target student body, and the level of technology available to these students, will influence how many of the available "bells and whistles" are used in a given course.

There are constantly new products produced for this market, and numerous tools that can be employed in an online course. Although no list can be exhaustive, the technologies listed below are some of the most commonly used today:

E-Mail

Electronic mail is a very common form of online interaction, and is present in virtually every distance education package. It is also used as an adjunct tool for communication between teachers and students in many "face-to-face" courses. E-mail is a delivery and receipt mechanism mostly for textual material, although other files, which could be textual or any other type, can be "attached" to the message. It allows educators and students to communicate with each other asynchronously, sending messages to individuals or groups easily and quickly. Messages can be written at any time, and can be read and responded to at any time. A file of e-mail messages sent and received is typically archived on the individual's computer.

Threaded Discussions

Threaded discussions are another form of asynchronous textual communications. An educator or student may post a message pertaining to a certain subject in a forum accessible to the whole class. Other participants can respond to that message or any of the responses, and so on. The evolution of the threaded discussion is displayed in hierarchical form to allow a participant to follow the discussion. A student or instructor can read the original message, the responses it generated, and the further comments generated by each of those responses. In this way, it seeks to recreate, in a time-independent environment, the flow of a classroom discussion while keeping a record of the discussion's progress.

Chat

The chat function provides a synchronous meeting place online. Students and instructors who are online and in this program can write messages back and forth in real time. As one student types a message, for instance, the text appears on the computer of all the other students present in the chat room. This technology allows for live discussion similar to classroom experiences. It is possible for the participants to keep copies of the chat session.

Whiteboard

A whiteboard program is one that provides a common space in which students and instructors can work synchronously. Similar in use to a blackboard in class, whiteboard technology can be used for display or collaboration. During a whiteboard session, each participant has a blank application on their screen, a "whiteboard." Any participant can then cut, paste, draw or write anything into this common space, and it will be immediately displayed on the boards of all the other participants. This technology is useful for group projects or planning sessions, which require students to collaborate on creating something. It can also be used in connection with a lecture delivered through streaming technologies, permitting the instructor to display images or text to the class as she lectures. Participants can save the contents of the board to their computer at any time.

Shared Applications

Like the whiteboard, a shared application can be used for display or collaboration. A shared application is a computer program like a word processor or drawing program that permits several people to use the program at the same time from different locations. The participant with the program to be shared (usually the teacher) opens it and specifies that he wants to share it. Demonstrations can be accomplished this way or, if the instructor specifies that the application can be used for collaboration, anyone in the class can also use the shared application. For example, all participants in a class session might have access to the same word processing program or graphic design program, and would work with each other within the application to create a product. In some implementations, the work that is done in the application can be saved or printed only from the computer of the person who shared it. For someone else to obtain a copy of the final product after collaborating, the person who shared it must send the file to the other participants.

Streaming Video/Audio

Streaming video or audio is similar to broadcast technologies, except that the transmissions are sent over a computer network. Instead of the receiving computer's waiting to receive an entire file of audio or video information before playing it back, the receiving computer begins to play back the file while it is still arriving over the network. Playback is done "on the fly," in other words. With enough network capacity ("bandwidth") the result is comparable to radio or television. In practice, however, the limits of the Internet's capacity today result in video images appearing small, with jerky movements. Sound quality is often quite good, though here again, the speed of one's connection to the Internet, and the congestion on the Internet at the time, make substantial differences in the quality of playback.

In common implementations today, streaming audio and video do not result in a complete copy of the entire transmission being placed on the user's computer, although a different implementation could be created that would do so. With appropriate equipment, such as cameras and microphones, the audio or video can also be two-way. This technology is used to deliver lectures to students, or hold class sessions with interaction.

Video/Audio Files

Video and audio files can be used to illustrate lessons or teach specific subjects. For example, a foreign language class might contain sound clips of different pronunciations of words, or a history class might integrate video clips of recorded interviews of war survivors with the lecture material. These files reside on the class network site for the duration of the class, and can be copied and downloaded by the students.

Course Management

Course management describes the infrastructure of the instructional content of the course. This could include the syllabus, written or recorded lectures, assigned reading, tests, and homework assignments. It generally involves posting material in common spaces on the network site, together with directions on how and when to access different portions of the material. For instance, an instructor might post a new lecture every week, with reading assignments, and a subsequent threaded discussion on the lecture. Or, she might choose to post all lectures and reading material at the beginning of the course, allowing students to read ahead, and organize chat sessions or threaded discussions every week on a different lecture. This information, once posted, generally remains on the course site for the duration of the class.

Links

Links provide a way for students to quickly access material not present on the course site itself. Links to other websites can be embedded in the text, or listed separately. For instance, a lecture on computer programming might include a link to an Internet website rating different types of software. Links may also transport the student to the university's library, where a student may access electronic reserves of material put aside by the instructor for that particular class.

Interactive CD-ROMs and DVD-ROMs

Some classes furnish students with a CD-ROM or DVD-ROM that interacts with the course website. These store large files, such as video, audio or animation, that would otherwise be posted on the websites. When the student clicks on the graphic or video clip in the course site, his computer obtains the file straight from the CD-ROM or DVD-ROM, instead of downloading it from the web page. This saves time, and also allows large files to be viewed with higher quality.

The above tools are generally used in classes that involve some form of instructor-student interaction. There are also tools available for self-paced independent learning-the latter-day parallel to video and audio tape courses that can be taken home and used at the student's convenience, with no interaction with a teacher. In the digital environment, computer-based training is a common form of distance education.

Programs on a variety of subjects can be obtained by the student from commercial vendors or in the course of instruction at an educational institution. The student reviews the material at his own pace, and tests himself on computer-generated exams. The programs themselves may contain a mixture of media, including video, audio, graphics and text. They could be contained in a CD-ROM, for example, downloaded from a network site, or accessed online. The student has little or no interaction with a teacher, although the student may send the results of the computer testing to an educational organization for grading or credit.

Technologies for protecting works

With the ever-increasing ability to transmit huge amounts of material quickly and easily over computer networks, copyright owners and users in all sectors recognize the need to provide security for that material. Many technology companies and content-provider groups are working to develop technologies for protecting works in the digital environment that will be viable in the marketplace. Industries are also collaborating among themselves in an effort to develop broadly-based, effective technological standards.

Technology can protect copyrighted works in many ways. It can restrict access to the work, restrict uses of the work and identify the terms and conditions of using the work. In some circumstances it can also find copies of the work on the World Wide Web and report their existence to the copyright owner, who can determine whether the copy is authorized. While there is a substantial degree of overlap in these technologies, they can be separated into technologies that limit access to works, and technologies that prevent or detect uses of works after access.

Each method of technological protection varies in its cost of deployment and degree of security. As a general matter, there is a correlation between these two factors: the more expensive and complex the mechanism, the more inviolate the material. If the expense is high, the material to be protected may not warrant the outlay. As a result, the stronger protections may be used to protect only high market value works.

Although many of these technologies are highly effective, none provides absolute certainty. Any code can be broken, and any mechanism can be circumvented, with enough effort and investment. The effectiveness of access control technologies in particular depends on the behavior of users, such as a student who is careless with his passwords or intentionally shares them with others.

The goal of most of these technologies is to provide a high enough level of protection that the cost of circumvention outweighs the value of access to the material protected.

Limiting Access

A range of methods can be used to control access to content. Educational organizations may limit access to students enrolled in a particular class or at a particular institution through several different methods used separately or in combination. Listed below are some of the most common methods used in the educational environment:

Password Protection

Password protection is probably the most common type of protection in educational settings, and most educational institutions seem to use some form of password protection to ensure that their distance education classes reach only registered students. Access is restricted by use of passwords or "logins," assigned codes used to identify an authorized user. These protection devices allow the institution to act as a gatekeeper, permitting only authorized users entry to shielded systems or select data. Each student can be issued a single password, which opens access only to a course for which the student has registered, or the student can be provided a different password for each class. Passwords typically expire at a predetermined time-the termination of the class, the semester, the school year, or the student's enrollment in the institution.

Firewalls

Both intranets and firewalls are common methods of protecting computer networks, and are used in many educational institutions. An intranet is an internal network cordoned off from public access by use of a firewall. Firewalls are created by a server, located between the intranet and the public network, which has been programmed to prohibit unauthorized users from accessing internal data. The firewall itself is not an access control mechanism; rather, it prohibits users from accessing the internal data by any means other than whatever access control mechanism the university has in place.

IP Addresses/Domain names

By screening for only specific IP addresses or domain names, it is possible to restrict access to a website or other content source to only those computers that are attached to a specific set of networks. This allows content to be restricted to machines on a specific campus. These methods of access control are somewhat limited in the distance education environment. Restriction by IP source address or domain name can be used to restrict access to members of an institutional community, but not to students registered in a specific class, since class registration does not correlate to either IP address or domain names. In addition, many distance learners do not work on campus computers, but work from home or some other place. Because they will not be working from addresses on the campus network, they would not be able to access the material.

Hardware Connections

Physically connecting hardware is another way to restrict the access of unauthorized users to transmitted data. In the digital environment, connecting computers together can create a system similar to the "closed circuit" television systems in which cables connect the transmitting sites to the receiving sites, effectively limiting reception to within the circuit. This manner of transmission is still being used for both broadcast and digital network transmissions. Where computers can be physically connected to each other, unauthorized access to the transmission can be avoided.

Encryption

While the use of intranets and passwords limits those who may enter or log on to a system, encryption technology limits access to information by protecting the information routed between a sender and a designated receiver. In an educational context, encryption allows instructors to send protected information which can be read only by students with the authorized decryption key. Encryption technologies are commercially marketed at a range of prices, depending in part on the level of protection. Encryption technology, in essence, encodes information from a sender into an unreadable form. Only an authorized receiver who holds the key to decode the information can access it.

Physical Control

Putting the content into a physical object, such as a CD-ROM, which is given only to authorized users is another method used to control access to information. A CD-ROM is a physical copy of digital information that is inserted into the computer when the user wishes to access such information. The work may be viewed on the screen, but resides in the physical disk. Access to that work is therefore limited to students who are in possession of the CD-ROM. Although the use of a CD-ROM has not traditionally thought of as a technological protection, using a CD-ROM as a delivery mechanism is more restrictive than posting a work on a website.

Technologies that control access are only part of the equation. Standing alone, they cannot control what happens to the work once it has been accessed. After an encrypted work has been decrypted, or a password-protected site has been logged into, the material is available for further use, including printing, downloading to computer memory, or electronic distribution. Technologies that affect the downstream uses of protected works are intended to address this gap. Some restrict use of the work, and others allow unauthorized uses to be detected.

Several alternatives exist for restricting use of a work once it has been accessed. Few of these technologies are yet in common usage. Several have just been released on the commercial market; others are expected to be commercially launched in the very near future; and still others are projected for release in the next year. The state of flux of this type of technology is high. As these technologies all represent different methods of addressing similar problems, it remains to be seen which, if any, will gain widespread acceptance and use with consumers and content providers. New ideas for addressing the same problems may also surface tomorrow.

Much attention is being focused on secure container/proprietary viewer technologies as a way to protect digitally transmitted works. There are a number of such technologies currently in the market or indevelopment, and some copyright owners are considering them as viable alternatives for selling and controlling works of high market value in the digital environment.

These technologies are often designed for a specific type of work (e.g., audio, video or text), and allow copyright owners to set rules for the use of their works. These rules are attached to all digital copies of the work, regardless of how they are further copied or distributed, and prevent anyone from making a use of the work that is not in accordance with those rules.

Basically, the technology works by encoding the digital work and wrapping it in a proprietary file format that can be opened only by software that reads and abides by the usage rules contained in the file. The file format contains the conditions of access and rules of use for the work. The conditions of access specify which users are allowed access.

The complementary software resides on the computer of the user. This software identifies the user and responds to the rules embedded in the container. It also acts as a viewer, allowing the user to see or use the content, filtered through the viewer, in accordance with the embedded rules. However, the content is never subject to distribution or copying in decrypted form. If the work is further disseminated, the proprietary file format moves with it, and the work cannot be accessed or used by anyone who does not have the proper viewer and authorization.

There are several examples of such technologies currently on the market, or in late stages of development.

Most are designed to handle one type of content, although there are products which offer protection for all type of works. Some examples are listed below. This list is illustrative only, and focuses on some of the technologies brought to the Copyright Office's attention during the hearing and comment process. It is not intended to be comprehensive, or to endorse any particular product or service.

Adobe Acrobat Reader: Acrobat is a system that includes a proprietary file format called PDF (portable document format), a reader and software to create the secure documents). The most recent version was released in late March 1999. The format is widely used in scientific and technical journals and many other electronic publications. Using Acrobat, the publisher can set privileges in the file that the Acrobat Reader obeys. The publisher may require the user to enter a password to view the document, and can permit or restrict printing, modification and cut and paste. The file format can accept text, graphics, Powerpoint slides and spreadsheets, and the new version allows more advanced access control mechanisms. Acrobat 4.0 is relatively inexpensive, selling for about $200 to the publisher. The reader software is free and is often distributed as a plug-in for browsers. Acrobat Reader is widely used today. It is primarily designed for printing high- quality copies of documents rather than as a mechanism for viewing documents on-screen.

Liquid Audio: Liquid Audio is a secure container technology currently used to sell recorded music files over the Internet. Liquid Audio both delivers content and accepts payment. It does not, at this point, allow specialization in the types of uses it permits or restrict. A customer using Liquid Audio has a limited number of choices-he can hear a sample, see the album cover, and sometimes read the liner notes. Then, if he decides to buy the recorded music, it is downloaded, marked with the buyer's unique player ID. Only software obtained from Liquid Audio and installed on the user's computer with a serially numbered identifier can open that file. After purchase, the buyer can listen to the recording as often as he chooses, but cannot copy or distribute it further.

InterTrust: InterTrust is one example of a secure container system for protecting all types of works. Works come in secure containers called "digiboxes" which are accessed and used through proprietary viewing technology on the user's computer, called the InterRights Point. Although not yet in commercial deployment, InterTrust began shipping system developer kits in June, 1998, and is in an advanced stage of development. The technology incorporates a permission system for obtaining authorization to use a work, a payment mechanism if a charge for such use is assessed, and a tracking mechanism, if desired andconsistent with privacy agreements, to monitor usage for the purposes of metered payment. It also allows a highly nuanced set of rules to be enforced.

Such technologies could be used in a digital distance education context. For example, the rules attached to a work through a secure container technology might provide that protected material could be accessed only by a registered student at a particular college, and that the student could view the work, and print out one hard copy, but could not save it to disk or distribute it to others electronically. A license fee, if any, could reflect these restrictions.

The student's viewer could then identify the user as a registered student, allow the student to see or print the work, but not allow the work to be sent through the viewer to the student's hard drive or e-mail system. If the information was being provided based on rules that required the institution to pay per use, the software could monitor the use for future accounting. This protection would apply to any kind of work and would persist in the work. The rules could also provide that after a certain time period, for instance a semester, the material would no longer be accessible. Secure container technologies that protect a range of works are not currently in use in distance education, however. As these are relatively new technologies, it is difficult to predict the level of investment required to create and operate such technologies within an educational system. Some developers indicate that pricing could be geared for educational institutions.

Streaming formats. Streaming technologies for video and audio are not technically mechanisms to protect content, but rather to deliver it. However, using advanced streaming formats for video or audio, no copy of the whole work is created on the user's computer. Because these technologies do not facilitate the making of copies, they can hinder downstream uses by the receiver of the transmission. Therefore, a byproduct of the properties of the delivery mechanism is that it offers some degree of protection against redistribution.

Low resolution data. Another manner to discourage downstream uses of protected works is to provide the works in a format that is not conducive to high quality reproduction or distribution. Low resolution digital copies can be provided to the user with less than the full complement of digital data, creating a copy of lower quality. Such a copy can be adequate for on-screen viewing but does not print well. This technology is currently used for marketing graphic images online, allowing a prospective user to view a low resolution copy of the work, but requiring a purchase in order to obtain a high-quality image. It does not appear to be in common usage in the distance education environment. This may be because it is difficult for instructors who rely on graphic images, such as graphic design or art teachers, to teach their classes effectively using low-quality images.

In addition to technologies that restrict the use that can be made of a work, technologies for embedding information in digital works to identify and track usage are also in development and use. Information may be attached to a work in a number of ways, from adding it to the image visually (e.g., a serial number at the end of a text) to integrating it invisibly in the digital data.

Since it is fairly easy to remove a visible identifier, the practice of digital watermarking, which does not permit easy removal, is growing. Digital watermarking is the technology of embedding information within the content of a digital file in a manner that is not ordinarily perceptible without the use of special software. A digital watermark does not hinder copying of a digital file, but the watermark will be present in the copy. Although it is possible to remove watermarks, it generally involves more than trivial effort and inconvenience, and some types are harder to remove than others. Digital watermarks are typically used to embed information in a digital file about the copyright, such as the identity of the copyright owner and the terms and conditions of licenses.

Users with the appropriate software can display this information and contact the copyright owner to clear rights to use the work embodied in the file. In general, it is easier to watermark some kinds of content, such as music and video, than others, such as text. The same digital watermark can also be used to detect unauthorized copying. There are two kinds of identifiers commonly used to track copying. The first type simply identifies the copyright owner, stating in effect, "I am owned by X." The second type identifies not only the copyright owner, but also the entity that licensed that copy of the work, for example through a serial number issued to each licensee.

Using commercially available software or services, these identifiers can be used as a search object to find unauthorized copies on the World Wide Web. A number of different programs have been proposed or are in use, known as "web spiders" or "net crawlers," which automatically search the web for incidences of these unique identifiers and report the information to the copyright owner. The copyright owner can then look at the location of the material and determine whether the use is authorized. If the type of identifier has been used that identifies the licensee, the owner can determine where the first unauthorized copy originated. Such programs ordinarily can only search material accessible on the World Wide Web, and not material stored on intranets, hard drives, or e-mail systems.

Significant and promising developments are occurring in all areas of technology involved in digital distance education. Although their outcomes are not certain, a few generalizations can be made. More efficient licensing mechanisms will continue to evolve and become more widespread. Delivery systems will become more sophisticated, more interoperable and capable of transmitting more material faster, making distance education even more varied and interactive.

Developments in technologies for protecting content are harder to predict. Here too there is reason for optimism. A number of technologies exist today that can provide effective technological protection for different types of works. Access control measures such as password protection are already common in distance education. Sophisticated technologies to prevent post-access uses of material are also a reality, although few are yet widely available. Some are in use in limited markets, some are in trial, and many are the focus of ongoing investment and development.

The use of open standards is beginning to emerge. In the near future it will be technically possible to protect works against both unauthorized access and dissemination with a high degree of effectiveness. It is an open question, however, whether these technologies will gain widespread usage and consumer acceptance. Many promising projects in the past have not passed that hurdle, due to factors such as cost, inconvenience, or difficulty of use. It is therefore difficult to forecast the extent to which these effective technologies for downstream protection will be available in practical form for use in digital distance education at any given point in time.

CHAPTER 2

Availability of Educational Technologies

During the 1990s, the availability of educational technology increased substantially at the school level. By 1999, most teachers reported having at least one computer in their classrooms, and over half of these teachers also had access to the Internet in their classrooms. Additionally, the majority of teachers also reported having these technologies available at home. Despite the gains in computer and Internet availability at school and in classrooms, approximately one-third of teachers reported that their classrooms had a single computer or a single computer connected to the Internet available in 1999.

The availability of technology was not equally distributed among schools with different characteristics. For example, teachers in schools with lower minority enrollments were generally more likely than teachers in schools with the highest minority enrollments to report having the Internet available in the classroom. Additionally, teachers in schools with lower poverty concentrations (based on the percent of students eligible for free or reduced-lunch) were generally more likely than teachers in schools with high minority concentrations to report having the Internet available in the classroom.

In 1999, the availability of technology in the classroom was related to teachers' use of that technology. For example, teachers who reported having more than five computers in their classrooms were more likely than teachers with fewer classroom computers to report using computers a lot for various preparatory activities.

Additionally, teachers who had more computers available in the classroom were generally more likely to report assigning students to use computers or the Internet to a large extent to conduct various tasks.

National Assessment of Educational Progress (NAEP) teacher survey, and the Current Population Survey (CPS) from 1994 to 1998. Data are also provided from the 1994 to 1999 FRSS school surveys on the percent of schools and instructional rooms with Internet connections. This background information is followed by more recent, detailed findings on the technology available to teachers and their students, taken from the 1999 FRSS survey on teachers' use of technology. Included are differences in the availability of computers and Internet connections by characteristics of schools.

Availability of Computers and the Internet

Measures of computer availability come in a variety of forms, including the percent of students who have varying numbers of computers available to them in their schools (NAEP), student-to-computer ratios in schools

(FRSS), the percent of students who have computer labs and portable computers available to them (NAEP), the percent of students who have computers permanently available in the classroom (NAEP), and the percent of students for whom computers are best described as available in computer labs or available in the classroom (NAEP).

Measures of Internet availability in public schools are similar, but typically focus on the percent of schools connected to the Internet rather than on the percent of students with the Internet available to them. These measures include the percent of schools connected to the Internet Availability of Technology for Instructional Purposes.

Number of computers available to students and student-to-computer ratios. Beginning in 1990, NAEP began collecting data from school administrators on the number of computers available to students in the school. Results from these surveys demonstrate a substantial increase in the number of computers available to public school students in their schools between 1990 and 1999. For example, the percent of fourth-grade students who had more than 76 computers available in their schools rose from 1 percent in 1990 to 33 percent in 1998.

Similarly, there was an increase from 8 percent to 51 percent of eighth-grade students and from 42 percent to 73 percent of twelfth-grade students during those years. According to recent FRSS data, approximately one computer was available for every six students in 1999.

Computer availability in labs and classrooms. Data are also available from the NAEP 1998 school survey on the location of computers in the school. For example, administrators indicated if the school had computer labs and whether computers were always available in classrooms. Additionally, administrators were asked if computers were available to be brought to classrooms for student use as a measure of portable computer availability.

The different types of computer availability (e.g., labs, available to be brought to class, classrooms) varied by grade-level in 1998. For example, among public school students, eighth and twelfth-grade students were more likely than fourth-grade students to have computer labs available. Conversely, fourth-grade students were more likely to have computers always available in the classroom than eighth and twelfth-grade students.

Teachers' reports of computer availability to students. In 1998, public school teachers of fourth-and eighth-grade students were asked to best describe the availability of computers for use by their students. Teachers reported whether: computers were "not available to students anywhere," computers for student use were "available in a lab," or varying numbers of computers for student use were "available in class."

According to their teachers, the majority of both fourth-grade and eighth-grade students had computers available to them somewhere in their school in 1998, either in the classroom or elsewhere in the school.

Specifically, percent of fourth-grade students and 49 percent of eighth-grade students had at least one computer in their classrooms, and 23 percent of fourth-grade students and 42 percent of eighth-grade students had at least one computer available in lab. Thus, 5 percent of fourth-graders and 9 percent of eighth-graders did not have computers available in their schools.

The FRSS also collected data on the percent of public schools and instructional rooms that were connected to the Internet as part of its school surveys between 1994 and 1999.

In 1994, a little over a third of all public schools were connected to the Internet. By 1999, availability had grown to 95 percent, with one computer connected to the Internet for every 9 students. The percent of instructional rooms connected to the Internet grew even more sharply during that time—whereas 3 percent of instructional rooms were connected to the Internet in 1994, 63 percent were connected by 1999.

The 1999 FRSS data indicate differences in student-to-instructional-computer ratios by such school characteristics as enrolment size, location, poverty concentration, and minority enrollments. For example, the smallest schools had a lower student-to-instructional-computer ratio than medium and large schools (4 compared with 6 each), as well as a lower student-to-instructional-computer-with- Internet ratio.

Rural schools had a lower student-to-instructional-computer ratio than schools in other locations. Furthermore, rural schools had lower student-to-instructional-computer-with-Internet ratios than urban fringe and city schools.

Additionally, there were differences in student-to-instructional-computer ratios by poverty concentration and minority enrollments in 1999.

Similarly, schools with the highest minority enrollments had a higher student-to-instructional-computer ratio than schools with lower minority enrollments. Differences by poverty concentration and minority enrollments were also present in student-to-instructional-computer-with-Internet ratios.

Schools with more than 70 percent of students eligible for free or reduced-price lunch had more students per instructional computer with Internet than schools with lower poverty concentrations. Similarly, schools with the highest minority enrollments had a higher student-to-instructional-computer-with- Internet ratio than schools with lower minority enrollments.

The highest poverty schools were also less likely to report having instructional rooms connected to the Internet than several other groups in 1997 and 1998. Between 1998 and 1999, all schools except those with the highest poverty concentrations reported an increase in the percentage of instructional rooms connected to the Internet. In 1999, 39 percent of instructional rooms at schools with more than 70 percent of students eligible for free or reduced-price lunch were connected to the Internet, compared with 62 to 74 percent of schools with lower concentrations of poverty.

Availability of Computers at Home

The availability of computers in teachers' homes is compared with that of adults in other occupations, and the number and ages of computers in the home are also given for the most recent year. Results from the 1994 to 1998 CPS indicate that the availability of computers in public and private school teachers' homes increased significantly between 1994 and 1998. Furthermore, elementary and secondary teachers were more likely to have a computer at home than adults in all other occupations in 1994 through 1998.

Additionally, in 1998, most teachers and adults in other occupations reported having computers that were three years old or newer. The CPS also collected data on public and private school students' computer availability at home in 1994 to 1998. According to these data, the percent of students who had at least one computer in the home increased from 36 percent in 1994 to 56 percent in 1998.

Finally, the relationship between computer availability in the classroom and teachers' computer-related activities is explored. Nearly all public school teachers reported having computers available somewhere in their schools in 1999. Eighty-four percent of public school teachers had computers available in their classrooms, and 95 percent of teachers had computers available elsewhere in the school.

Number of computers in the classroom. In addition to asking teachers if they had computers available in the classrooms, the 1999 FRSS survey also asked for the number of computers available in the classroom. As previously indicated, most public school teachers reported having at least one computer in their classrooms in 1999. Thirty-six percent had one computer in their classrooms, 38 percent reported having two to five computers in their classrooms, and 10 percent reported having more than five computers in their classrooms.

Differences in school and classroom computer availability by school characteristics. Teachers' computer availability in 1999 varied by several school characteristics, including instructional level, enrolment size, location, minority enrollments, and poverty concentration. Elementary teachers were more likely to have computers in their classrooms than secondary teachers. Teachers in schools enrolling less than 300 and 300 to 999 students were more likely to have computers in their classrooms than teachers in schools with the largest enrollments.

Last, teachers in schools with 21 to 49 percent minority enrollments were more likely to have computers in the classroom than teachers in schools with 50 percent or more minority enrollments. There were also differences among teachers who had varying numbers of computers in the classroom. Not only were some groups of teachers less likely to have computers in their classrooms, but they were also more likely than other teachers to have only one computer in their classrooms.

Teachers in secondary schools were more likely to have one computer than elementary teachers, and less likely to have two to five computers than elementary teachers. Computer availability also varied by school size. For example, teachers in schools enrolling 1,000 or more students were more likely to report having one computer in their classrooms than teachers in schools with less than 300 students.

Teachers in schools enrolling 1,000 or more students were less likely, however, to report having two to five computers than either schools enrolling 300 to 999 students or schools enrolling less than 300 students.

Sixty-four percent of public school teachers who reported having computers in their classrooms also reported having Internet availability in their classrooms in 1999. Ninety percent of teachers who reported having computers available elsewhere in their schools also reported that the Internet was available elsewhere in the school.

Number of classroom computers connected to the Internet. Among the teachers who reported having computers available in their classrooms, approximately one-third had no computers connected to the Internet and about half had one computer connected to the Internet. It was less commonly reported that teachers had two to five computers connected or more than five computers connected to the Internet.

Differences in school and classroom Internet availability by school characteristics. There were differences in overall Internet availability (in class or elsewhere in the school) and in the number of classroom computers connected to the Internet by several school characteristics. For example, secondary teachers with computers in their classrooms were more likely to have Internet availability in their classrooms than elementary teachers.

Internet available on the computers that they did have in their classrooms. Furthermore, among teachers who reported having computers available elsewhere in the school, secondary teachers were also more likely to have Internet availability elsewhere in the school than were elementary teachers.

Additionally, teachers in schools located in towns were more likely to have Internet availability elsewhere in the school than teachers in urban fringe schools or city schools.

Similarly, teachers in schools with lower minority enrollments were generally more likely to report this availability elsewhere in the school than teachers in schools with the highest minority enrollments. Internet availability also varied by poverty concentration.

For example, public school teachers in schools where 11 to 30 percent and 31 to 49 percent of the students qualify for free or reduced-price lunch were more likely to have the Internet available in the classroom than teachers in schools with 71 percent or more students eligible. Teachers in lower poverty schools were also generally more likely than teachers in the highest poverty schools to have Internet available elsewhere in the school. Specifically, teachers in schools with less than 11 percent, 11 to 30 percent, and 31 to 49 percent students eligible for free or reduced-price lunch were more likely to have this availability than teachers in schools with 71 percent or more students eligible.

As with overall Internet availability in the classroom, the number of classroom computers that public school teachers reported as having Internet connections varied by instructional level and minority enrollments, but not percent of students eligible for free or reduced-price lunch. For example, secondary teachers were more likely than elementary teachers to have either one computer connected to the Internet or more than five computers connected. In addition, teachers in schools with 6 to 20 percent minority enrollments were more likely than teachers in schools with 50 percent or more minority enrollments to have one computer connected to the Internet. Moreover, teachers in schools with less than 6 percent minority enrollments were more likely to report having two to five computers connected than teachers in schools with 50 percent or more minority enrollments.

E-mail Availability in School

Public school teachers were asked whether e-mail was available in their schools in 1999. Among those who reported having any computers available in their schools, 74 percent indicated that e-mail was also available. E-mail availability varied by location of school, minority enrollments, and poverty concentration.

Rural teachers were more likely to report e-mail availability than city teachers. Moreover, teachers in schools with lower minority enrollments were more likely to report that e-mail was available than teachers in schools with the highest minority enrollments.

Furthermore, teachers in schools with less than 11 percent, 11 to 30 percent, and 31 to 49 percent students eligible for free or reduced-price lunch were more likely to have e-mail available than teachers in schools with more than 70 percent eligible students.

The 1999 FRSS teacher survey also asked teachers if they had the Internet available at home, and if their school had a network that they could access at home. Sixty-three percent of public school teachers reported having the Internet available at home in 1999.

In addition, 27 percent reported that their school had a network that they could use to access the Internet from home. There were several differences in teachers' availability of computers and the Internet at home by school characteristics in 1999. For example, teachers in schools with 1,000 students or more enrolled were more likely to have a computer at home than teachers in schools with less than 300 students enrolled.

Similarly, teachers in schools with 300 to 999 students enrolled and schools with 1,000 or more students enrolled were more likely to have Internet at home than teachers in schools with less than 300 students enrolled. Teachers in urban fringe schools and schools located in towns were more likely to have the Internet available at home.

Teachers in schools with the highest minority enrollments were less likely to report that the majority of their students had computers at home than teachers in any other schools. In addition, teachers in the lower poverty schools were more likely to report that their students had computers at home than teachers in the highest poverty schools.

Classroom Instruction and Computer Availability

Teachers' reports of assigning students to use computers or the Internet for various instructional purposes differed by the number of computers in their classrooms. For example, 59 percent of teachers with one computer in the classroom reported not assigning students to use computers or the Internet to solve problems or analyze data, compared with 40 percent of teachers with two to five computers and 23 percent of teachers with more than five computers.

Conversely, teachers with more than five computers in their classrooms were most likely to report assigning problem solving or data analysis computer work to a "large extent," followed by teachers with two to five computers and teachers with one computer.

Technology Use in Schools and Classrooms

According to CPS data on Internet use, frequency of technology has been used somewhat infrequently by public and private school teachers in past years, but use of this technology is growing. For example, in public and private schools, the percent of elementary teachers who used the Internet at work rose from 23 to 33 percent between 1997 and 1998, and the percent of secondary teachers who used the Internet at work increased from 28 to 43 percent. In the 1999 FRSS teacher survey, public school teachers were asked if computers, the Internet, and e-mail were available to them in various locations, and if available, the extent to which they used them.

Among teachers who reported that computers were available in their schools, 99 percent indicated that they used computers either in their classrooms or elsewhere in the school. Additionally, among teachers who indicated that computers with Internet connections were available in their schools, 96 percent used the Internet from their classrooms or elsewhere in their schools. Furthermore, at least three-fourths of teachers with e-mail availability used it at school.

Frequency of use by location of technology. The 1999 FRSS teacher survey asked teachers how frequently they used computers and the Internet in two locations: the classroom and elsewhere in the school. Of the teachers who reported having computer availability in their classrooms, nearly all of them.

In addition, among teachers with Internet availability in their classrooms, 88 percent reported using this technology. Of those teachers who reported Internet availability elsewhere in the school, 70 percent indicated using it. Teachers were more likely to use the Internet in the classroom than elsewhere in the school, and they were also more likely to use it to a large extent in their classrooms than elsewhere in the school.

Furthermore, of the 74 percent of teachers reporting e-mail availability in the school, 77 percent used it at least to some extent. Teachers were significantly more likely to use computers in the classroom than elsewhere in the school, and they were also more likely to use them to a large extent in the classroom than elsewhere in the school.

Frequency of use by number of computers available. The 1999 FRSS teacher survey also asked teachers the number of computers and computers with Internet connections that were located in their classrooms. Overall, teachers with more computers in their classrooms used them more frequently than teachers with fewer computers in their classrooms.

For example, 62 percent of public school teachers with more than five computers in their classrooms used them to a large extent compared with 43 percent of teachers with two to five computers and 28 percent of teachers with one computer in their classrooms.

Similarly, teachers with more than five computers with Internet access in their classrooms used the Internet from the classroom more frequently than teachers with fewer computers with Internet access in their

Furthermore, teachers with computers in their classrooms used computers elsewhere in the school more often than teachers with no classroom computers. At least one-fifth of teachers with computers in their classrooms used computers elsewhere in the school to a large extent compared with 10 percent of teachers with no computers in their classrooms. Similarly, teachers with one or more than five computers connected to the Internet in their classrooms used the Internet elsewhere in the school more often than teachers without classroom computers with Internet connections.

Twenty-four percent of teachers with more than five classroom computers connected to the Internet and 12 percent of teachers with one classroom computer connected to the Internet used the Internet elsewhere in the school to a large extent, compared with 7 percent of teachers with no classroom computers connected to the Internet.

Frequency of use by teacher and school characteristics. Differences were found in the frequency of teachers' use of computers, the Internet, and e-mail by school and teacher characteristics. Teachers with fewer years of teaching experience were more likely to use computers, the Internet, and e-mail to a large extent at school than their more experienced colleagues.

For example, 48 percent of teachers with 3 or fewer years of teaching experience and 45 percent of teachers with 4 to 9 years of experience used computers at school to a large extent, compared with 33 percent of teachers with 20 or more years experience. The pattern is similar for Internet and e-mail use. Furthermore, teachers in schools with minority enrolments of 6 to 20 percent were more likely to use e-mail to a large extent than teachers in schools with the highest minority enrolments.

According to the 1997 CPS, 69 percent of adults employed as secondary teachers (either in public or private schools) and 67 percent employed as elementary teachers (either in public or private schools) reported using computers at work. Both are significantly lower than such occupations as librarians, editors and reporters, and college faculty, and the percentage of elementary school teachers who reported using computers at work was lower than that of those employed as lawyers and judges and real estate and available in the classroom" analyses. Teachers who reported that computers with Internet connections were not available to them in the classroom were excluded from the "Number of computers with Internet connections available in the classroom" analyses

Students' Technology Use at School

In the 1999 FRSS teacher survey, public school teachers were asked how often students in one of their typical classes used computers and the Internet—"not at all," "rarely," "sometimes," or "often"—in various locations (i.e., in classrooms and elsewhere in the school).

Overall technology use. Eighty-eight percent of teachers with computers available in their schools reported that their students used computers either in the classroom or in computer labs, libraries, and media centres in 1999.

Frequency of use by location of technology. Approximately seven out of ten teachers reported that students used classroom computers; however, a higher percentage of teachers reported that students used them elsewhere in the school. Thirty-four percent of teachers reported that students used the Internet in the classroom; however, a higher percentage of teachers reported that students used the Internet elsewhere in the school.

Twenty-six percent of teachers reported that students used classroom computers often, and 28 percent of teachers reported that students used computers elsewhere often. Six percent of teachers indicated that students used classroom computers with Internet access often, and percent of teachers indicated that students used computers with Internet access elsewhere in the school often. Sixteen percent of teachers reported that students used other technologies, such as distance learning 3 through the Internet and other interactive media.

Frequency of use by number of computers available. Overall, teachers with more computers or Internet availability in their classrooms reported that they and their students used these technologies more frequently than teachers with fewer computers in their classrooms.

Similarly, 33 percent of teachers with more than five classroom computers connected to the Internet reported that students used them often compared with 6 percent of teachers with one classroom computer connected to the Internet. Additionally, teachers with two to five classroom computers connected to the Internet were more likely than teachers with one such computer to report that students used the Internet often. Furthermore, teachers with computers in their classrooms reported that students used computers elsewhere in the school more often than teachers with no classroom computers.

At least one out of three teachers with computers in their classrooms reported that students used computers elsewhere in the school, compared with one out of six teachers without a classroom computer. Teachers with more than five computers connected to the Internet in their classrooms were two to five times as likely as teachers with one or no computers with Internet connections to report that students used the Internet elsewhere in the school.

Additionally, teachers with one, two to five, and more than five computers with Internet access in the classroom were more likely than teachers with no computers with Internet access in the classroom to report that their students used the Internet elsewhere in the school. Frequency of use by teacher and school characteristics. Students' use of technology, as reported by their teachers, varied by teacher and school characteristics. For example, elementary teachers were more likely than secondary teachers to report that their students used computers at school to any extent. However, secondary teachers were more likely than elementary teachers to report that their students used the Internet at school to any extent.

Furthermore, teachers in schools with lower minority enrolments were generally more likely than teachers in schools with the highest minority enrolments to report that students used the Internet at school. Sixty-four percent of teachers in schools with less than 6 percent minority enrolments and 65 percent of teachers in schools with 6 to 20 percent minority enrolments reported that students used the Internet in school compared with 53 percent of teachers in schools with more than 50 percent minority enrolments.Similarly, teachers in schools with lower poverty concentrations were generally more likely to report that students used the Internet at school than teachers in the highest poverty schools.

Seventy-one percent of teachers in schools with less than 11 percent of students eligible for free or reduced-price lunch, 63 percent of teachers in schools with 11 to 30 percent of eligible students, and 66 percent of teachers in schools with 31 to 49 percent of students eligible for free or reduced-price lunch reported that students used the Internet at school compared with 50 percent of teachers in schools with 71 percent or more students eligible for free or reduced-price lunch.

Current Frequency of Technology Use at Home

Experience using a computer or the Internet may improve teachers' and students' technology skills and increase their level of comfort with technology, regardless of whether the use is at school or at home.

In the 1999 FRSS teacher survey of technology use, teachers were asked if a computer, the Internet, or a school network through which they could access the Internet were available to them at home. If they were available, teachers were then asked about the extent to which they used them. Because the FRSS did not ask similar information about students, data from NAEP and CPS are used to describe students' technology use at home.

Teacher Use of Computers and the Internet at Home

The 1997 CPS indicates that for public and private school teachers, 83 percent of elementary teachers and 89 percent of secondary teachers used home computers to any extent when they were available. This compares with 74 percent of adults in other occupations with computers at home who used them to any extent. Two years later, the 1999 FRSS teacher survey indicates that 98 percent of public school teachers with computers at home used them, and about half of the teachers used them to a large extent.

Teachers' Internet use at home significantly increased between 1997 and 1998 for both elementary and secondary teachers. According to the 1997 CPS, 35 percent of all elementary teachers with computers in their households and 44 percent of all secondary teachers with computers in their households reported using the Internet at home.

Home Internet use also increased between 1997 and 1998 for adults in other occupations with computers in their households, from 37 to 51 percent. The 1999 FRSS teacher survey indicates that nearly all public school teachers with the Internet available at home used it, and about two-fifths of teachers with home Internet access reported using it to a large extent.

The 1999 FRSS teacher survey also inquired about school networks that teachers can access at home. Fifty-six percent of teachers used this technology when it was available. Home use by teacher and school characteristics. Public school teachers' use of computers and the Internet at home varied by their years of teaching experience.

For example, teachers with 3 or fewer years and those with 4 to 9 years of teaching experience were more likely to use their home computers to a large extent than teachers with 20 or more years of teaching experience. Similarly, teachers with 3 or fewer years and those with 4 to 9 years of teaching experience were more likely to use the Internet at home to a large extent than teachers with 10 to 19 years and those with 20 or more years of teaching experience.

Public school teachers who used computers for instruction during class and teachers who assigned projects that required their students to use a computer were more likely to use computers and the Internet at home to a large extent than teachers who did not use these technologies for such purposes. For example, 54 percent of teachers who used computers for instruction also used home computers to a large extent, compared with 43 percent of teachers who did not use computers for instruction. Likewise, 52 percent of teachers who assigned projects requiring students to use computers also used home computers to a large extent, compared with 37 percent of teachers who did not assign such projects.

Structural Change and Educational Technologies

Every revolutionary technology starts with a whimper. Its full revolutionary bang is realized only later after fundamental structural changes are made to accommodate the new technology.

Steam engines were first put on sailboats to solve a persistent problem: time wasted in the doldrums. When there was no wind, the steam engine was fired up and used only until there was enough wind for sailing. Steam was initially viewed as a solution to a problem for sailboats, not as a replacement for them. But, of course, in the end sail power vanished and steam permitted faster, larger, safer, all-metal ships that could move goods faster and much more economically.

There are countless examples like these in the history of technology, where a new technology is first used to address a narrow problem within the existing order and only later overthrew the old order. The delay is inevitable because structural changes are needed for the new technology.

In the case of ice machines, universal access to electricity and lower costs through mass production were needed before everyone could buy a refrigerator. In the case of steamboats, deeper harbors, new construction techniques, and railroads to supply coal and remove cargoes were needed before large, steel steamers made sense. There is dawning realization that the current economic boom has technology to thank because of the structural changes it has caused in business. Productivity is up because technology means that fewer managers are needed, businesses are far less hierarchical, and financial markets have been democratized.

In spite of the decades that computers have been around and their current high use in schools, we have yet to see the revolution they could cause in learning. Educators are still delivering block ice made by ice machines, still using steam only in the doldrums. This is because business competition rewards improvements while education is organized to conserve and pass on the best of the old.

In addition, education is highly labor-intensive, and the cost of labor has been bid up by the buoyant economy. We are, nevertheless, overdue for a surge in education performance driven by the technology, as soon as we are willing to make the necessary structural changes. This will profoundly improve education.

Before jumping into the specifics of the educational change that technology will cause, it is important to understand where we are in the information revolution and where it is going. We must look at not only the technology itself, but also the structural change society must make to accommodate it.

Moore's Law

One indicator of this ongoing change is "Moore's Law", an observation made by Gordon Moore in 1965, several years before helping start Intel. Moore observed then that the number of transistors on a microchip was doubling every 18 months.

This kind of exponential change applies to the entire information industry, not just computer chips. Similar exponential increases in performance will be seen in all components: displays, keyboards, and media.

Experts expect these changes to continue 10-20 more years, but no one really knows. The result might be a trillion-fold increase in performance since 1965 and a million-fold increase from today. It is impossible to predict what new applications that these improvements in the underlying technology will enable, but it is certain that the structural changes necessary to exploit them fully in education will take additional decades. We are helping write the script of the opening scenes of the most dramatic play educators have ever witnessed.

A direct consequence of the ongoing revolution described above, in only a few years computers will be very inexpensive and ubiquitous. Each person will own several and have easy access to more—all able to communicate over the Internet. Toys, TVs, phones, pagers, handhelds, and general-purpose computers will have access to the net. Wireless access will become common and switching between wired and wireless connections will be effortless.

Any indicator of technology access in the U.S. will show a similar behavior over the next decade, showing a gap that dwindles into insignificance as prices drop. This is because information technologies are relatively low-cost and dropping. Unlike jets, reactors, and rockets, computer and network technologies are "democratic technologies." Like TVs, VCRs, calculators, and radios, information technologies are soon to be ubiquitous.

The vanishing of the digital divide defined as access to technology in the U.S. will not, of course, rectify the deplorable inequities in U.S. schools. Because of inadequate funding and more difficult working conditions, too many poor schools will not use the technology well, will be unable to maintain it, and will provide fewer opportunities for their teachers to exploit it. The result will be continued poorer education in many poorer schools.

The cost of access to technology will not contribute significantly to this persistent, essentially political, problem. If anything, the technology, by providing free access to increasingly valuable resources, will have a leveling effect that will tend to reduce the gap.

The situation throughout the world will be essentially similar, with the exception of much of central Africa. In most parts of the world, the huge digital divides that exist today will close as access becomes ubiquitous.

Many countries already exceed the U.S. access to technology and even developing countries see the importance of computer and networking technologies. Ubiquity will be accompanied by increasing reliance on the network to synchronize data. You want your personal mailing list to be on your cell phone and TV computer. If your student masters multi-digit subtraction in school, her educational games at home should take advantage of this and her parents should be informed. Data collected on a colleague's handheld computer should be available on your portable.

All these feats of synchronization will happen automatically and effortlessly through the network. The location of the data will not matter; you may choose to store your data on your main computer's hard drive, a server in Budapest, or for security, your personal smart card. It is quite likely that each learner will have a net-based educational profile that can change as the individual learns. This is how a student's progress can be monitored, shared among different computers she uses, and reported, as appropriate, to parents and others responsible for her education.

Leapfrog, a maker of educational toys, is already planning a line of mass-produced products based on this principle. An online educational profile is a potential privacy bombshell. Everyone will want tight and secure control over who looks at grades, test scores, progress, weaknesses, essays, and preferences.

Technology can solve this, though, through some combination of encryption, a smart card that physically controls the data, and related software.

Characteristcs of Technologies

Before projecting educational uses of technology, it is useful to summarize the unusual characteristics of networking technologies. These characteristics have led to the Internet's impact on commerce and have dictated the structural changes needed to exploit fully the technology in business. We can look at these for hints about the similar structural changes needed in education.

The power of the Internet is that almost anyone can contribute to it and there are ways to find anyone's contribution. This could lead to the junk and misinformation drowning the relatively rare pearls. This is unlikely, however, because the decentralization also supports self-appointed annotators and collectors of links that provide vetting and review functions. In fact, this self-publishing feature has unleashed tremendous human creativity.

Every corporation, government agency, school, town, association, group, museum, and individual wants to put their best on the net. One of the most dramatic manifestations of the ethic of sharing that the Internet has spawned "open source". The open source movement is highly decentralized, but rallies around the idea of the GNU Public License (GPL) as an alternative to conventional copyright protection.

The GPL states that anyone can use the source code without charge providing the user protect any improvements with the GPL license. Companies can sell the software, providing that they continue to make the source freely available. The result is that the source code stays public and keeps getting refined. GPL software can be better than software simply placed in the public domain, because the terms of the GNU license stop anyone from grabbing the public code and making it proprietary. The result is code that everyone is motivated to review and improve the code. Code that survives tends to be lean, elegant, stable, and free.

Initially, open source software focused on the Linux operating system software, but this is changing rapidly. The people shaping the effort insist that system software is only the beginning. Because open source development is the best way to create reliable and elegant software, they are certain that most software will eventually be distributed under the GPL.

The open source motto is "Software is meant to be free." They may be right. Already the open source idea has reached far beyond Linux. In addition to the

Netscape browser, there are now open source spreadsheets, word processors, a presentation package (like PowerPoint), and gimp, an image manipulation program that is better than PhotoShop. The open source software idea is beginning to appeal to corporations, because it offers an inexpensive way to incorporate free software into their product and get better product support than they can afford to hire. All Netscape's code is open source, as is much of the next generation Macintosh operating system. IBM is installing GNU/ Linux into some computers.

The U.S. has led the world in Internet use and implementation, but the rest of the world will overtake. The largest growth in Internet use over the next few years is expected in Latin America and Asia.

According to Global Reach, currently, 49% of the 335 million Internet users worldwide are non-English speaking. In 2003, the 670 million non-English users will be more than double the number of English-speaking users. There are already 18 million Chinese users and there might be 125 million in 2003.

While these projections are open to question, the general trend is not. The majority of the educated population of the world along with most of its institutions will be strutting their stuff online in a few years. These new users will bring a rich collection of new resources and interests to everyone.

The world's books, art, data, pictures, animations, music, simulations, poems, and much more will be available. Collaborators, collectors, mentors, advisors, and consultants for every imaginable topic will be a few clicks away.

Unfortunately, all kinds of undesirable resources will also be increasingly available. There will be the entire world's junk, smut, hatred, violence, stupidity, superstition, and insanity. Every form of vice and bad habit will be represented, too. Even more viruses will be circulated and more attacks on computer systems mounted. In addition, the Internet is rapidly becoming commercialized.

Some of the most amazing services are available free, subsidized by advertisers. Computers, email, storage, faxing, news, music, search engines, financial data, and much more are available free because they are paid for by advertisers. There is no point in avoiding the Internet because of these undesirable aspects.

We have to face the problems and learn to minimize them. One of the skills we will need to learn is how to find the good, reliable stuff for ourselves and youngsters in our charge while avoiding the bad.

Software tools have revolutionized business and hold the key to breakthroughs in education as well. Software tools are general-purpose, flexible applications that you can apply to your specific needs. In business, spreadsheets, presentation software, and communication tools have empowered workers to make decisions and marshal resources without the need of levels of hierarchy.

Design tools have sped the development of new devices and software, increasing productivity. In education, tool applications will also lead increases in learning and productivity in all disciplines. Literacy tools are revolutionizing the language arts, design tools have broad application across the arts and engineering, and conceptual tools will completely change all technical and social science learning.

For a tool to be educational, it needs to be part of an instructional design. Software can help there, too, especially if the tool and pedagogy are separated. All these new tools will be too expensive to develop from grants and corporate investments but open source can solve this problem.

Technological tools will become increasingly important in teaching literacy and second languages to children, adults, and special students. Over the next few years, there could be important breakthroughs in technology-enhanced literacy learning, because there is a convergence of developments: Voice recognition. Research is underway on computer recognition of children's voices and speakers with accents. This ability can be used to recognize reading, judge accuracy, and shape pronunciation.

The coming inexpensive ubiquitous computers will give all learners could access to inexpensive literacy tools. Networking. Students can use networks to find an audience for their work, a community of interest and collaborators for their investigations. Game machine quality simulations. The incredible graphics capacity of new 128-bit game computers may create the emotional impact that can capture any learner's imagination.

Computer generated material can continuously evaluate student reading and writing, reducing wasted testing time. Inexpensive handhelds will soon be able to exploit these developments to provide interactive voice generation and recognition. With embedded assessment, the material can advance as fast or slowly as the learner needs. Playful content will be available for young readers while vocationally-relevant material will better suit adults.

While human intervention, motivation, and supervision will be necessary, the ubiquitous technology and software tools will greatly reduce the amount of teacher time required for literacy instruction. The bulk of the reading, listening, and correcting can be shifted to the computer, resulting in huge productivity breakthroughs. This could result in literacy gains worldwide, while decreasing the advantage families have that can find the time to read to their children extensively.

Software tools that support creativity are one of the great gifts of computers. Design tools for Web development, robot programming, and music composition are available and increasingly used in education.

Design as a subject is under-represented in schools today. Design is at the core of engineering, architecture, many technologies, and art. The success of many businesses depends on their technical and artistic designs. Successful designs depend on planning, testing, knowledge, and artistic sensibilities.

A central goal of education should be to foster these skills. Perhaps the root of the lack of emphasis on design education has been a perception that design consists of two parts that each seem to be problematic. Its creative side has lacked expression outside art class and may seem too intuitive and lacking in theory that would give educators something to teach and evaluate.

Design's other face is technical and may be judged as too difficult and abstract for pre-college students. Again, computers and networking provide tools that can solve both problems. Tools for Web authoring, image manipulation, drawing, and 3D rendering allow students to be creative and share their creations with others.

There are meaningful concepts and skills students need to acquire in all areas of design that can be gained through the use of these tools. On the techncial side, design and modelling tools can help students understand the technical ideas underlying design without having to master abstract mathematics or complex programming languages.

Logo and its extensions—Boxer, StarLogo, NetLogo, and Microworlds—represent one important set of tools that make design education feasible at the precollege level. Logo has gotten a bad rap in education because it was ahead of its time. It was embraced by pioneers as THE answer to "computer literacy" and subsequently widely adopted for all the wrong reasons. The resulting backlash has left many educators with a persistent bad taste.

This is unfortunate, because the Logo idea and the work of its inventors from MIT's Media Lab have articulated a new approach to education based on design. Schools need to increase greatly their emphasis on teaching design. This will require fundamental structural changes in education. New goals will have to be articulated, standards articulated and courses developed.

Profound learning happens when models student build to simulate reality meet data students collect. The combination of sophisticated data acquisition from probes and Internet databases with models that can be compared to data, can lead treakthroughs in learning.

For example, "Kinetic Molecular Theory" is commonly taught in middle school science. The usual approach is to introduce a series of postulates roughly along the lines of "in an ideal gas, there are no attractive forces between molecules. These molecules act as point particles that bounce off on another like pool balls without loosing energy." It is then asserted that these postulates predict the gas laws, but no justification is provided for this assertion. This must leave most students quite perplexed. First, the "ideal" gas is clearly incorrect; its molecules are not point particles, and there are forces between them.

Students can change the size and forces between atoms and measure the resulting relationships between pressure, temperature, and volume. They can see how these macroscopic properties emerge from atomic properties and interactions. The gas laws are obvious consequences this system, as is phase change, latent heat, and crystal structure. Using probes, the gas laws and latent heats predicted by the model can be quickly verified in real systems.

Instead of the apparent complexity and inaccessibility of KMT as usually treated, this technology-rich approach clarifies the underlying concepts and relates the non-ideal properties of real liquids and solids to an ideal gas. The entire vocabulary of "ideal gases" and "KMT postulates", as well need to assert without proof that there is some relationship between the two, becomes unnecessary. The result is that students learn at a deeper level without encountering the confusion and apparent contradictions inherent in the usual approach.

We can teach ideas like KMT more deeply because the computational power of modern computers give a new way to understand abstractions. Until computers, the only way to relate the postulates of KMT with the gas laws was through formal mathematics and the advanced undergraduate level. Students had to wait that long for a fully satisfactory understanding.

Even then, the formalism is so difficult, students often fail understand the science. Thus, educators at the precollege level have no choice but to present the material as facts that must be memorized and taken on faith.

The combination of computer-based data collection and modelling can cause a breakthrough in student learning because it provides an alternative and more accessible way of understanding abstract concepts. Instead of using complex formal methods, a higher degree of student understanding can be gained by interacting with a suitable model.

Deeper learning accessible to more students can be expected in all the sciences, mathematics, technical fields, quantitative social sciences, and business. Genetics, macro-economics, chemical reactions, evolution, space shots, fire fighting, the stock market, global warming, epidemics, urban planning, and much more can be better understood through DOING it with a model than reading about it or trying to understand it through mathematics. The result will eventually be that many more abstract concepts will be taught at the pre-college level. This is essential to our economy because it is exactly these abstract ideas that fuel our economy.

This breakthrough will have profound effects on special students. For some, this will be liberating, for others, the increased emphasis on conceptual understanding will be make math and science even more baffling. The shift will probably catch many special educators napping who rely heavily on software for drill and practice.

Since few special educators are strong in the concepts of science, math, and technology, becoming more concept-focused will put more pressure on classroom teachers to adapt to the needs of special students. A major structural change will be needed to take advantage of modelling and data analysis tools. Teachers will be needed who have a deeper understanding of their subjects and who know how to teach these concepts with the appropriate use of educational technologies.

Educators at all levels will have to adjust to the increased learning that is possible, including the test makers, standards setters, colleges, and schools of education.

Unfortunately, tools have proven hard to use in education. Makers of educational tools have always had a problem: do you produce a simplified version for the learner or one with every conceivable feature for the expert? The stripped-down version is hard to sell because some other tool will have more features and get a better reputation. On the other hand, a full-featured tool is hard for teachers and students to master.

One alternative is to add educational content into the tool. One form of this is "scaffolding", a variety of helping strategies that fade away as the user becomes more expert. Context-sensitive help, that annoying assistant-in-a-window in Microsoft Office, and tutorials are other strategies to address this problem.

The alternative is to separate the tool from the pedagogical software. The tool should have no pedagogical strategy built into it. Instead, it should have "hooks" to a second software package we call Pedagogica. This is an application that is designed for controlling tools to achieve learning objectives. Pedagogica can control how many options the user sees, sense what users do with a tool, and interact directly with the user. By changing the script that Pedagogica executes, it can provide help, scaffolding, or the full-featured tool. This means that the educational strategy is not determined by the tool and can be changed to adapt to the needs of the curriculum and students.

One of the benefits of a tool like Pedagogica is that it can provide embedded assessment. The script that controls what material is presented to students needs to make judgements about what to present. This requires assessment of student learning that can be embedded in the tasks.

For instance, consider the script that is used with a model of atoms in a box to teach that pressure and temperature are proportional under some conditions. The script can observe whether a student has considered enough conditions to make this prediction. It can suggest new conditions and then observe what generalizations the student makes.

Watching and guiding this kind of problem solving will give the software detailed data on what the student knows and can do. These data are essential for the software to provide useful guidance. It also provides invaluable assessment data. The software can tell what a student has done, how long it took, how many blind alleys were pursued, and how persistent these errors were. We are building a graphical interface for Pedagogica in which the script closely resembles a concept map.

This will allow educators to think in terms of concepts and understandings that are familiar and closely related to the mental models we hope student will develop. Pedagogica is very much a work in progress, but something like this is needed to unleash the educational potential of general-purpose tools. We need to reach broad agreement on the need to separate pedagogy from tool applications and for the technical specifications of the "hooks" tools need to communicate with something like Pedagogica.

Open source provides the best way to develop the needed educational tools. Open source software exists outside the normal commercial distribution channels, but supports commercialization and a flourishing service industry. Businesses, from startups to IBM and Microsoft, surprisingly have learned to embrace open source. On the other hand, education has essentially ignored it.

The only significant educational open source is a version of Logo by Brian Harvey and a productivity package, Star Office, that could see broad use in education. NSF sponsored research sometimes yields valuable educational software that is free during development, such as various versions of StarLogo, Image, and Biologica.

Technically, these are not open source, since their developers retain the right to commercialize the software eventually. One of the reasons for the paucity of open source educational software is that the open source may need to be nurtured through enlightened self-interest. Once there was a critical mass of open source system software it was in everyone's interest to expand that core. If a hacker needed a Linux driver for an obscure printer, he or she would write it and be bound, under the terms of the GPL, to contribute it to the common good. There was also recognition from gurus for solid, well designed contributions.

This suggests that educational open source could provide general-purpose languages, tools and simulations, especially if it was seeded with a critical mass and there were recognition for important contributions. The critical difference between the current open source system and its possible application to education is the consumers. In the former case, the consumers are techies who can use the software with little or no assistance or ancillary information.

In education, the consumers are nontechnical teachers and will need curriculum materials and professional development to use open source software. Perhaps this is not as large a distinction as it appears, however. As the interest in open source has expanded, intermediaries have sprung up who consolidate and test open source software, provide documentation, and make it self-installing so that even nontechnical users can install it.

Open source educational software is certain to receive increased interest as other countries begin to explore educational applications of technology.

For instance, open source educational software is already beginning to make an impact in Mexico. A university-based group had developed a graphical user interface for Linux and some applications that are being distributed free to all schools. Compared to the U.S., education in most other countries is more centralized, more closely connected to higher education, and far less likely to spend money on commercial software. As a result, there will be funding for software that will be distributed freely to schools.

Since each country will have similar needs, it makes sense that software development be shared, and open source offers the best alternative. If funding is provided to seed and coordinate an international educational open source movement, we could unleash the kind of global creativity that has created and expanded open source software for business.

The educational open source effort should concentrate on general-purpose tools with standardized hooks for pedagogical controllers like Pedagogica. If educational open source started this way, then enlightened self-interest could accelerate the process. General-purpose tools could find worldwide application.

Scripts would adapt the tools to the special needs and goals of specific countries and regions. If tools and scripts were open sourced, then every developer would have a powerful incentive to adhere to open source rules. There is certain to be thousands of bright, creative programmers throughout the world who would be thrilled to have the chance to contribute to improved education everywhere.

The resulting educational tools and pedagogical scripts could be far more sophisticated and extensive than anything we can hope to develop through grants and business investment. A coordinated effort to seed open source development could yield a rich harvest of educational applications that would be far better and broader than current software and completely free.

This vision of learning that relies on tools guided by scripts using open source software leaves little room for traditional textbooks. Current science texts for high school courses can exceed 1,000 pages and weigh more than a portable computer. They require, with associated materials, years and millions of dollars to develop.

The texts must include every topic any significant sub-audience might want, while avoiding potential controversies. This huge investment results in high prices, the use of copyrighted content, and the inability to include public domain materials. This approach to curricula yields heavy, expensive books that are frozen in time.

Even if they include software and Web pages, these ancillary materials only begin to scratch the surface of what is possible. They certainly fail to include sophisticated modelling and data collection tools. The textbook-based approach to teaching science is too limiting and too inflexible; it belongs to the prior century. The realization of the power of technology requires a structural change in curriculum design and dissemination.

The value of a textbook and its ancillary materials is that it represents a coherent aggregation of resources and educational activities. Technology can provide the benefits of aggregation while avoiding the costs, inflexibility of a text and constraints of needing to own all the materials. This aggregation can be achieved through a flexible online curriculum framework with "slots" for modular digital materials that adhere to high standards. These slots might feature lab activities, software-based investigations, discussions of videos, structured investigations of a model, or research projects.

The modules that fill the slots will come from sponsored educational R&D, academic researchers, teachers, or businesses. This modular structure would ensure far faster integration of materials originating in R&D labs that now often languish without a publisher. It is often incorrectly assumed that relying on digital materials isolates learners and deprives them from opportunities for direct, hands-on learning. It is certainly possible and desirable to include in the curriculum collaboration and discussions both online and in-class and also give students ample opportunities to hands-on learning using probeware, off-line projects, activities, and field studies.

A complete curriculum would consist of a framework with all slots filled with excellent, highly interactive, research-based materials that take full advantage of data and modelling tools. The result will be richer than a text, because it will provide interaction, computation, and collaboration in the context of learning resources. A complete set of curriculum materials of this sort for a course might be produced with the same care as current texts, but be based on modules that can be easily modified or substituted for other materials as they become available. States and districts could modify the materials to fit their standards and interests.

The modules requiring specialized labs, software, or technology could be modified to fit whatever a school has implemented. Some modules would be free, others would be licensed with a small fee in lieu of the textbook purchase costs, going to the authors. Implementing these online curriculum resources will require that all students have easy access to computers and networking. This is, however, no reason to fail to start exploring this alternative to texts now. By the time high quality, fully integrated digital curriculum frameworks can be developed, filled, and tested, the technology will be ubiquitous.

Tools, even with excellent pedagogical software, are not going to revolutionize education alone. These critical elements need to be integrated into courses students take. The process of changing courses can be excruciatingly slow. Effective online courses are can accelerate this process by disseminating improved materials and techniques while also creating competition that can stimulate change.

Effective courses are able to engage students at a distance in collaborative, activity-based learning, in small groups guided by trained facilitators. The best approaches use asynchronous, two-way technologies that rely on carefully designed activities, good evaluation strategies, and communities of learners facilitated by online discussions.

They also take advantage of the computer for simulations, models, data collection, calculations, mentoring, and creations as appropriate. Well-designed online courses are at least as good as face-to-face courses and are usually more inclusive and better designed. Only a fraction of the online courses fit these characteristics, but time will weed out the many poorer designs.

Online Courses for Students

Online courses for secondary students are exploding. At the advanced level, high school students can enroll at colleges and universities, one-third of which now offer Internet-based courses for credit. Although slower than post-secondary education to exploit the power of online courses, high schools are increasingly offering effective online courses to their students. Secondary education has lagged colleges and universities in using online courses because few schools have the incentives or resources to offer courses themselves.

Post-secondary institutions have strong financial incentives to increase income from tuitions from distant students. High schools are chartered to serve a community and cannot increase their income by stealing students from other districts. In addition, post-secondary institutions tend to be larger and better able to afford the investment required to create effective online courses.

The answer for secondary education is to form cooperatives of schools to share online courses. If each of 200 schools teaches a section of an online course, then all of their students have access to a pool of 200 course sections. Rather than competing for students in a zero-sum game, everyone gains from this form of sharing. The costs are low, too, because schools in a cooperative don't have to pay tuition. If they balance out the number of seats they create through offering courses with the number of seats their students need, there are no new instructional costs. Of course, there are administrative costs in running the cooperative and training the participating staff, but these are less than tuition.

The Department of Education's Technology Innovation Challenge program and resulted in the Virtual High School. Through four years of operation, we have demonstrated how such a cooperative can work. We have learned how to prepare teachers to offer online courses, how to keep standards high, and how to handle all the problems of scheduling, registration, orientation, and accreditation. The conclusion by independent evaluators from SRI International is that students, teachers, unions, and administrators love the VHS online courses. They are personal, challenging, and interesting.

The courses offer quality, flexibility, and scope that is invaluable. Their range of topics is a godsend to students with specialized interests. Tiny schools can offer a range of courses that is the envy of larger schools not in the program. At least two smaller schools were saved from oblivion because of this. The cooperative nature of the VHS is a key innovation that will prove essential in the long run.

Some states, such as Florida and Kentucky, are beginning to offer online courses funded at the state level. These are doomed because they represent a major shift of instructional costs and control from the community to the state. In the end, the states cannot afford this shift and communities and unions will not permit it.

Similarly, for-profits or entrepreneurial colleges cannot expect to earn more than a tiny fraction of secondary school instructional costs because schools will want to keep those funds in the community. A larger district, however, should be able to sustain effective online courses in its high schools because it can act like a cooperative, sharing among schools instructional resources in the form of online courses.

Once the idea of online courses takes off, it could force some much-needed change. Advocates of vouchers and charter schools hope that the competition that their innovations introduce into education will provide incentives for all schools to improve.

Cooperative online courses actually create a far more intense pressure to change, but without the competition. Once schools can offer hundreds of high quality online courses, parents and students will have little tolerance for substandard face-to-face courses. There will no excuse for courses that do not use technology well, that are not carefully designed, or are out-of-date.

Students will protest with their feet and parents will demand access to the better online courses. Online courses could be the quickest way to disseminate new instructional approaches that make full use of modelling and data tools. At first, these new approaches will attract only a fewstudents. The strength of online courses, however, is that they can reach thin audiences—those adventurous students willing to try a new approach.

As data accumulates about the power of these alternatives, there will be demand for additional sections. The creation of educational cooperatives is an example the kind of structural shifts that are needed to exploit the information technologies. To exploit the power of online course, it is not sufficient simply to offer some courses. A set of economic, political, and practical problems must be solved which seem to demand cooperative sharing of courses.

Online Courses for Teachers

Effective online courses can revolutionize teacher professional development (TPD). They are able to deliver focused and timely assistance to teachers whenever they need it. Online teacher professional development during the academic year allows teachers to experiment with the new materials and approaches advocated in a course and then discuss the results with their colleagues.

Inherently, the costs for effective online TPD are lower than face-to-face courses and workshops because they avoid transportation, food, and meeting expenses. One of the most exciting current developments in TPD is the use of online interactive video case studies in online courses. The technology is nearing the capacity to handle video on demand, at least in short segments. This allows to imagine that large numbers of videos of exemplary teaching could be made widely available. It is well known that video case studies, properly supported, are far more effective for teacher than hours of abstract discussions or readings of how to teach. A video shows an entire environment, illustrates how to organize classroom space and time, and how respond to students' typical issues.

Online video case studies could be made highly interactive by linking them to lesson plans, typical student work, relevant standards and assessments, background content, expert commentary, teacher reflection, and moderated online discussion groups. As appropriate to the topics, there will be links to relevant tools, simulations, and implementation guidance. At any point, the user could stop, replay, jump ahead, or dive into the rich surrounding content.

Using interactive case studies in online course will be much richer than typical workshops that use case studies. The online teacher will be in charge, able to control the pace and depth of the experience. The privacy of the experience will permit teachers to acknowledge their content weaknesses and brush up on their understanding of content and technology. On the other hand, the online discussion areas will encourage collegiality and reflective sharing around focused, relevant issues.

The rapid changes in standards, assessment, content, curricula, and educational technologies create a massive need for ongoing teacher professional development. Technology itself puts new burdens on teachers. It is increasingly clear that every school will have a unique and rapidly changing combination of computers, networking, and software. Teachers cannot rely on textbooks to provide software and network resources coordinated with the text because they cannot be sure what technology will be available.

Consequently, the task of integrating technology is left to teachers. Teachers need detailed and specific help in adapting to these changes and new responsibilities. One teacher might want ideas for modelling software to use in eighth grade mathematics, while another might be looking for curricula that integrate conflict resolution into fifth grade. A high school biology teacher might be looking for some background in chemical bonding that is now in the standards. It is very difficult for schools to provide high-quality professional development opportunities for their teachers that are so specific.

Online courses, on the other hand, can reach thin markets with excellent courses designed by the best people in the field. While enough teachers to make up a workshop from one school are unlikely to need the same highly focused course, it is likely that a critical number can be found across the country on almost any conceivable topic.

To make this point, the University of Montana's NTEN project started with a course on teaching general relativity in high school offered by experts in the field. The regularly filled the course with 25 teacher participants. Dropouts have been a persistent problem in online courses.

Many teachers who are enthusiastic about online courses and praise them for what they have learned, fail to complete their courses. One exception has been the courses we offer in the VHS that are a prerequisite to teaching in the VHS. Here, unlike many TPD situations, successful completion is an absolute requirement for continuing in the project.

The problem is that teachers are incredibly busy and are seldom given released time for online TPD. In addition, there are seldom strong incentives for completion. The upshot is that even conscientious teachers tend to stay enrolled just long enough to get the materials and main ideas and then leave. This means that online courses should be short and highly focused and that successful completion should well rewarded.

Teachers should be able to select exactly the content they need and be able to absorb it in minimal time. What is needed, then, is the development of very large numbers of targeted online short courses for teachers that make liberal use of video case studies. These should be a half-semester long and accredited by a rigorous, external body. Schools need to expect their teachers continually to complete short courses that fit into the school's master plan for TPD, provide released time for the courses, and link advancement to successful completion.

We have begun to explore these ideas in a one-year pilot program just funded by the Department of Education called Seeing Math. With our partners COMAP and TeachScape, we will produce online case studies and short courses for teachers focused on grade 4-5 mathematics.

We are hopeful that this project will demonstrate the power of interactive video case studies and short courses that use them. A much larger effort is needed, however. Hundreds of case studies and short courses are needed to meet the diverse needs of teachers. This suggests cooperatives, designed along the lines of the VHS. If every district in a 200 school cooperative contributed a short course on a topic for which they had expertise, then teachers in all the participating schools would have 200 short courses to choose from. This would result in better use of existing PDF funds; the only new cost would be for the short course development and the administration of the cooperative.

Again, we see structural changes are needed to exploit the technology. In addition to the high bandwidth and modern computers needed for video-on-demand, full exploitation of the technology for TPD demands new cooperatives and accreditation functions, local support for online learning, and increased reliance on ongoing TPD.

Designing and offering courses online requires skill, knowledge, and discipline. The reason there are so many poor online courses is that teachers and entrepreneurs assume that this is an easy task for any teacher. To fill the need for disseminating the knowledge we have gained, we created "metacourses", online courses about online courses.

For instance, in the VHS course we have developed two that are central to the success of the project. The first is a yearlong 125 hour course about designing, creating, and offering a VHS course. The second is a one-semester course on how to offer an online course. As part of a different project, we have developed "Moving Out of the Middle", a popular course on facilitating online courses.

The nation needs many more secondary teachers trained in online courses. If we can get to college students who are making career choices, the opportunity to teach online might help attract more well qualified students into teaching. Being able to teach online can solve the problems of two jobs for married students. The ability of one spouse to teach online vastly simplifies the choice of location and opens more options for the other spouse.

In addition, online teaching is likely to be well paying because the online teacher can accept the best job anywhere. The opportunity to earn more and telecommute anywhere might be deciding factors for attracting outstanding students interested in teaching but discouraged by pay and working conditions. As a start in this direction, we have offered the one-semester VHS metacourse to preservice students. We have long dreamed of offering virtual internships in the VHS for preservice teachers, but have yet to find funders that idea.

Schools of education and licensing agencies will have to agree that online teaching is realistic option for students and that there are important things to learn about online teaching. This is likely to take decades without a concerted research and development effort.

In short, schools need to undertake major changes to fully exploit technology. Students will need increased access to technology. This will make it feasible to rely more on tool-type applications. Realizing the potential gains in learning will greatly strain schools. Teachers will need increased professional development in both content and the use of technology. Online courses will provide models for how to do this along with new opportunities for professional development. Online courses will also provide the spur of competition.

Students and parents will demand face-to-face courses of the same quality available online. If schools cannot meet that demand, they will loose students to home schooling or alternative schools better able to exploit the technology. Funding agencies could greatly accelerate the changes needed to realize these dreams.

Small studies are needed to find out what technology-enhanced learning is possible under ideal conditions. Large-scale, longitudinal experiments are need to work out the bugs and document the gains in student learning that are possible. Funding should be provided to develop and disseminate the needed online professional development and the training of online facilitators through metacourses. Most importantly, concentrated funding is needed to seed an international educational open source effort. Schools and funders need to realize that fundamental structural changes are needed.

CHAPTER 3

Information Technology in Education

According to a survey of information technology use in higher education in US, an increasing integration of computing related activities into college courses. This survey reported that three-fifths of undergraduate courses utilised electronic mail and two-fifths made use of World Wide Web (WWW) resources. Parallel to this trend is the growing number of colleges and universities instituting requirements for student computer ownership. This survey also reported that many of the schools implementing the requirement did so to guarantee that all students had access to the same computing resources. Surveys of teacher education programs seem to show trends that are similar to other higher education programs. While some statistics are available for teacher education programs as a whole, little research has been done in this area that focuses on technology education.

For example, does the strong emphasis on technology in general in technology education teacher preparation programs make it more likely that majors in these programs would own a computer than, say, a social studies or mathematics pre-service teacher? Apart from the actual ownership of the computer, are students in other education majors likely to utilise their computers differently in the course of their studies? These become important questions when assessing whether different teacher education programs are meeting local and national mandates for computing literacy.

While nearly all national teacher education organisations have called for some elements of computer competency, technology education has logically put computing and information technology literacy front and center.

The College of Education at North Carolina State University (NC State) has been consistently upgrading its technology infrastructure and integration of computing into the curriculum as a response to campus-wide and national trends as well as new technology competency requirements for current and future teachers. Though every faculty member in the College has a computer and four computer labs are available for both student use and instruction, there are still unanswered issues concerning reasonable expectations faculty members can make concerning student computer access and familiarity of different software tools when developing instructional materials for use by students.

In the Fall of 1999, the College of Education at NC State undertook a survey of its majors in all disciplines, including technology education, to gain an accurate look at many of these issues surrounding the use of computers and information technology. The researchers were not only interested in the level and type of computing activity going on in the college and within the technology education program, but also whether it was justifiable to treat all logical groupings of students as having equivalent access and experience with computing tools.

The faculty and administration wanted to know if computing needs differed with respect to certain demographic elements such as gender, age, and ethnicity. The researchers identified three principal areas on which to focus the study. First was the extent to which students owned computers and how they used these computers for school, work, and leisure activities.

A survey instrument was designed to gather information on the computing issues of interest. Computer ownership was determined by asking whether the respondents owned their own computer and, if so, how old it was. The age of a computer can be roughly equated to its capability. Determining the age of the computer was thought to be a simpler and seemingly more reliable way to determine the capability of a computer than asking about specific features of the machine about which the responding students may not be knowledgeable (i.e., RAM, hard drive capacity, CPU model and speed, etc.).

The instrument also measured computer usage. Frequency and duration are the most common scales used to measure usage. Previous observations of student computer usage in the College revealed that the duration of individual sessions on the computer were highly variable. Therefore, frequency would not likely to give a good measure of usage. For that reason, duration was used as the operational definition of usage. These computer-based applications were considered to reflect basic computer competencies. They included electronic mail, the World Wide Web (WWW), word processing, presentation graphics, databases and spreadsheets, and statistical analysis.

As of the Fall of 1999, the College of Education (then called the College of Education and Psychology) had 1695 undergraduate and graduate majors. The instrument was mailed to a stratified, random sample of one third of these majors (565). Since several of the programs had small numbers of students, the stratification was by department rather than program. A second stratum was class level. Of the 565 surveys mailed, 23 were returned as undeliverable. A total of 190 surveys were returned by students, for an effective return of 35.1% of the original mailing.

A second survey instrument was developed that mirrored the college-wide instrument. This instrument was sent to majors in the technology education program after the college-wide assessment was completed. A total of 54 (63%) of the 86 technology education majors in the College responded to the survey. In order to compare between technology education majors and other education majors within the College, information on other undergraduate education-related majors was abstracted from the initial college-wide survey.

Breaking down the College majors by class and area, 417 of the 1695 majors were in undergraduate teacher education programs. About one third of the total (139) of these undergraduate teacher education majors were part of the original survey sample. Of these, 111 were teacher education majors in areas other than technology education. Thirty-five (31.5%) of the 111 non-technology education majors in the initial survey sample had responded.

The majority of respondents from undergraduate technology education majors were white males attending college full-time. The majority of undergraduate respondents from other education majors within the college were white females attending college full-time.

The majority of respondents were between ages 19-21. Among the technology education respondents, not one reported being 18 or younger, while 37% of other education majors responding were 18 or younger. Also, more technology education respondents reported being 22 or older (35.1%) than other education majors (22.9%) within the College. Overall, 87% percent of all education majors indicated they have a personal computer they own and use. Eighty four percent of technology education respondents own a personal computer, compared to 91% of the students from other education majors within the College.

Most computers owned by both sets of respondents were between one and three years old. Computer ownership levels were analysed to see if any significant difference or interaction existed relative to the variables of academic major, gender, or race. Using an ANOVA test, no significant differences nor interactions were found. Likewise, the researchers found no significant interaction between technology education majors as a group and those in other majors. No interaction was found between computer age and either gender or race.

Also, no significant difference in computer age based on major, gender, or race was found. However, a significant positive correlation was found between the age of student and the age of the computer for the total population that participated in the study.

The second part of the instrument assessed the number of hours each week the students spent using a computer for school, work, and leisure and the extent to which they used their own computer or one available elsewhere. As mentioned earlier, computer use for work meant that the students were being paid for the time they were using a computer. The researchers compared differences in total computer use between major and class level using an ANOVA test. No significant differences or interactions were found in total computer usage between major and the class level (e.g. sophomore, junior, senior).

Likewise, there was no significant difference in total use by gender or race. Computer usage was then re-grouped into the three component parts of school, work, and leisure and the ANOVA applied again. No significant interaction or difference was found based on major or class level for either school or work computer usage.

Table 1
Average Hours Per Week Spent on Computing Activities

	Class Level	Tech. Ed	Other Ed
School	Sophomore	8.75	9.33
	Junior	8.50	5.25
	Senior	10.8	4.58
Work	Sophomore	3.57	1.83
	Junior	2.60	0.00
	Senior	2.27	1.66
Leisure	Sophomore	10.26	9.83
	Junior	7.75	1.50
	Senior	2.81	0.91

Although there was no significant interaction in leisure usage by major nor class level, a significant main effect was indicated for leisure usage by class level. Post-hoc analysis showed that this was between seniors and the other years. This trend also revealed itself in a significant negative correlation between leisure usage and age. No significant difference in leisure usage was found based on race or gender, nor was there any interaction with gender and class level or major.

Seven computing areas were identified in the initial study as being regularly used within the College: e-mail, world wide web, word processing, databases/spreadsheets, statistics, presentation graphics, and technical graphics(CAD). This study compared the time per week that technology education majors spent in these seven areas compared to students in other majors.

Using the ANOVA, no interaction or significant difference was found in the use of e-mail, the World Wide Web, or word processing by class level, major, or gender.

Table 2

Average Hours per Week Spent in Selected Computing Areas

Computing Area	Tech. Ed. Majors	Other Ed. Majors
E-mail	3.90	3.77
WWW	7.73	5.48
Word Processing	3.66	4.81
Presentation Graphics	2.24	0.25
Database/Spread Sheet	1.50	0.53
Statistics	0.12	0.32
Technical Graphics (CAD)	6.41	0.03

Although no interaction was found for the hours spent each week using presentation graphics between class level and major, a significant main effect in use of presentation graphics was found between majors with technology education majors using presentation graphics software more hours per week than other education majors. Though this two-way ANOVA did not reveal significance for class level, a one-way ANOVA on class level by itself did show a significant difference.

No significant interactions or differences were found between majors or class level for database/spreadsheet, or statistics usage. Although, no interaction in CAD usage between major and class level was found, a significant main effect in CAD usage between technology education majors and other education majors was found.

The results of this study showed surprisingly similar trends in computer ownership and usage between technology and non-technology education majors. These similarities were maintained when the education majors were broken down based on gender or race. From the demographic data, it is clear that males continue to dominate technology teacher education at NC State. This is in contrast to a majority female population in the other education majors. At the same time, females tended to own and use computers at the same level as male students.

Interestingly, there was a considerably higher level of computer ownership among the respondents in this study compared to what Brown reported. Even though computer ownership was not required, a large majority of students in general owned computers and the proportion was even higher among technology education majors (though the difference was not significant).

The lack of consistency between this study and the Brown study might be explained by socioeconomic differences between the two samples or by differences in support within the institutions. Understanding the barriers to ownership is important since ownership improves access to computer resources and this, in turn, influences the computing literacy of pre-service teachers.

The age of the computer is related to what students can achieve with it and the extent to which their experience is positive. The computers that technology education majors used were, in general, older than those of non-majors. Older students tended to own older computers. This is likely due to the fact that students purchase a computer when they first enrol in the university and keep this computer until they graduate. The fact that technology education majors are often transfers from other majors may explain why they are older, on the average, than non-majors. Correspondingly, this likely would cause them to spend more years earning their degrees and thus might explain why their computers are older.

The age of a computer provides a relatively good benchmark to judge the readiness of the machine to run current software. Given the hardware demands of the latest graphics, CAD, and multimedia software that technology education majors are expected to use, these students are likely to be disadvantaged if their computer is more than two years old.

A new computer ownership plan is being implemented by the College of Engineering at NC State that will have students lease computers and be able to trade them in after two years. A similar plan should be considered for technology education students. This study revealed little difference in total computer usage between technology education majors and other majors within the College. Likewise, there was little difference in usage among class levels. While there seemed to be greater overall usage by technology education majors than by other education majors, and by sophomores compared to other class levels, these differences were not significant.

Only when specific applications were analysed did significant differences occur.

The fact that education majors in nontechnical areas were making use of computers as much as technology education majors is indicative of the pervasiveness of computing activity in all curricular areas and in the work performed by students outside of school. On the other hand, it could be argued that the technology education program at NC State has failed to integrate computers to the extent that one would think, considering the nature of the of the discipline. A closer look at the differences in computing usage among major, class level, and type of activity might explain some of these findings. For both technology and other education majors, sophomores were clearly the heaviest users of computers. This difference was in large part due to the high amount of leisure time spent with the computer.

Sophomores and juniors from all majors engaged in significantly more leisure activity than seniors. While the interaction was not significant, the drop-off of leisure time spent using a computer between the sophomore and junior year for non-technology education majors was much more precipitous than it was for technology education majors. What is unclear is whether this drop-off was due to changing curricular demands as students move through school or whether, in fact, it might be revealing a micro-generational change in lifestyle. That is, younger students tend to integrate the computer more fully into all aspects of their daily life, including their (self-defined) leisure activity.

A significant negative correlation between leisure usage and age seems to support this latter theory. Another element of support for this notion comes from the significant negative correlation that was found between e-mail usage and age, since e-mail can be used for a wide range of non-academically-related activities.

Also of note, though not significant, is the reverse trend in use of the computer for school activities between technology education and other majors. While the amount of school-related activities increased between the sophomore and senior years for technology education majors, it dropped for other education majors. A closer look at the curriculum content of all the education programs might reveal the root of this differential trend. For example, the computer literacy instruction for all students could have been concentrated during the sophomore year.

When looking at specific types of software used by education majors, some interesting differences in usage emerged between technology and other education majors with respect to class level. Technology education majors used presentation graphics and CAD (computer-aided design) software significantly more than other education majors. This difference would be expected regarding CAD since it is such an integral part of a technology education curriculum. An explanation for the increased use of presentation graphics software among technology education majors is, however, is less obvious.

Unlike CAD, presentation graphics software is meant to be used as a general communication tool. As such, one would expect to find similar use among virtually all majors. It appears that students in other majors should be given increased encouragement and opportunity to use presentation software as part of classroom assignments.

Certainly presentation graphics software would be an essential element of computing literacy initiatives for pre-service teachers. Clearly, the use of these software tools and their integration into assigned activities would be a significant influence to their use in the future by an aspiring teacher. Technology education does seem to be doing a better job in this area than the other teacher education programs at NC State University.

In addition to showing differential levels of usage between majors, the use of CAD and presentation graphics differed by class level. Seniors were more likely to use CAD and presentation graphics than were lower level students.

Not surprisingly is a parallel, significant positive correlation between CAD and presentation graphics and age. In this instance the researchers were less inclined to point to the generational influence mentioned earlier as an explanation. Instead, the increased use was due to the fact that project-based activities and the presentation of their outcomes are more common in upper level courses at NC State and many other universities.

Looking at other application usage patterns, it is worth noting that technology education students seem to be making more use of the WWW, while other education majors were using word processing more. These differences were not significant, however.

More important may be the synergistic use of internet-based activities as shown in the significant correlation of WWW and e-mail usage for all education majors. Also significant is that e-mail and WWW usage is not significantly different between male and female students, regardless of major or class level. For those students who are connected to the internet, these tools go hand in hand.

Whether increased usage of internet-based tools such as the WWW and e-mail is good or bad is highly dependent upon how individual instructors integrate these tools into their courses and how students apply them in the course of their studies. The internet is a rich source of information exchange, but all information sources both electronic and paper-based must be used and evaluated based on their quality and their relevance to the academic tasks at hand.

The results of this study clearly indicate that computer ownership and computer usage was pervasive in the College of Education and Psychology in the Fall of 1999. This pervasiveness was independent of major, class level, gender, or race.

The predominantly white male technology education majors did not differ from other majors in terms of their overall usage of computing resources. It was only in the more specific analyses that differences were found between technology education and other education majors. Overall it appears that differences in computing use may be due more to the age of the student than to their major or gender.

It is risky to generalise the results of this study beyond NC State University in the year 1999. Computers and their application by students continue to evolve at a rapid pace. Institutions of higher education differ dramatically from one another, as do the programs within them. What was found at NC State may not hold true in other technology education programs due to a myriad of factors that were not controlled in this study.

However, the regular conduct of national surveys of technology education and other education programs are needed so that longitudinal trends can be observed. Such studies can be key elements in helping the technology education profession provide for the computing needs of its students and to set benchmarks for comparison. The computer has become a tool that is essential for all educators and this is especially true for technology education.

Online .Technology Education

As university level technology education programs begin to offer more online classes and degree programs, some current face-to-face technology education professors may be in the position of developing online offerings. Because online education can overcome some traditional barriers related to time and place, there may be special interest in the development of online graduate programs that could serve professionals who might find it a better option than leaving their work and home to establish residency at a university. Planning instruction for a new group of students using a new delivery method should be informed by the perceived needs and preferences of the target population.

Because of the ability to provide information from a large number and wide variety of respondents, the survey technique was chosen over other typical needs assessment data gathering methods, such as interviews, focus groups, and on- site observations. A survey instrument was developed consistent with the five typical stages of needs assessment survey development noted by McClelland: content definition, composing the survey, pilot testing, revision, and gaining approval to distribute the survey. Some of the instrument's content was developed based on the technological literacy standards released by the International Technology Education Association only weeks before the survey. A preliminary questionnaire was then developed, following recommendations by Gupta on the writing of training needs assessment instruments (i.e., Determine the types of data to be collected. Determine data sources. Involve experts. etc.)

During the development of the instruments, content and survey specialists were consulted. Content consultants included technology teachers, undergraduate and graduate technology education students, and professors in technology education. Two technology education professors from universities other than the hosting university were consulted specifically because they had recently conducted national surveys in technology education.

Two instructional technologists were also consulted, one of whom had recently used the survey software for dissertation research. Finally, two survey specialists from the hosting university's assessment office were consulted regarding the format of the instruments and coding of the results. Pilot testing occurred throughout the development period. Subjects included one undergraduate technology education student, one graduate technology education student, and five technology teachers. During the final round of pilot testing, all subjects seemed to interpret the meaning of the questionnaire's items and the formatting of their response as intended. After pilot testing, a revised instrument was prepared for delivery by mail and online.

In May, 2000, following human subjects protocol approval, 3,203 questionnaires were mailed with a cover letter and a postage-paid return envelop to all professional and student members of the International Technology Education Association (ITEA). A parallel online version of the questionnaire was available as an alternative, and cited in the mailing. The questionnaire included items on demographics, computer use, learning needs, and the educational appeal of online instruction.

As of July 20, 2000, 923 usable questionnaires were received (including 111 submitted online) for a response rate of 29%. This was nearly double the response rate from a needs assessment survey of engineering educators. Most of the respondents indicated they were professional members of ITEA, with only 8% indicating they were student members (the remainder did not respond to this item.) The most typical occupations of respondents were high school technology teacher (38%) and middle school or junior high school technology teacher (29%); ten percent noted they were university technology teacher educators, and 5% and 2% were undergraduate and graduate technology education students, respectively.

Most respondents (57%) indicated that the master's was their highest degree completed; 25% indicated the bachelor's, and 12% indicated the doctorate. Only 145 respondents (16%) had ever taken a course online. Thus, the results of this survey must be seen as describing the perception of online education, rather than experience with online education. When asked about their use of the internet, 829 respondents (90%) noted that they personally used the internet to learn about some aspect of technology. This indicated a high level of readiness to engage in non-formal distance learning.

Developers of online offerings should be aware of the computer resources available to their distance education students. More respondents reported using a PC regularly both at work and at home, than a Macintosh.

Many respondents reported using Microsoft Office and using the internet. The use of digital still and video technology was not as common, and was greater at work than at home, probably due to the cost of the equipment and its presence in many technology education laboratories.

Most respondents (63%) indicated that they used a 56K modem at home and most (57%) used T1 internet connection at work. These responses may seem to indicate that the majority of respondents have access to typical computer resources, including at least a 56K modem. However, online educators are cautioned against developing online instruction that is only appropriate for a fraction of potential students, even if that fraction does constitute a majority. Instead, accommodations for students with lesser technological resources should be devised.

Table 3. Percent of respondents reporting regular use of selected technology (n=923)

Technology	Location	
	Home	Work
Email	82%	85%
Internet	82%	86%
PC	76%	81%
MS Office	74%	81%
Digital Camera	30%	53%
Macintosh	27%	38%
Online Chat	14%	6%
Digital Video	12%	25%

Technology education professionals who are potential students would be well served if ITEA coordinated and facilitated access to education in these areas. This would also serve the needs of this association in ensuring that the content standards are understood and applied.

Some of the more traditional areas received greater interest than some of the newer areas, as seen by comparing means for "manufacturing technologies" and "construction technologies" with those of "agricultural and biotechnologies" and "medical technologies." However, there are multiple reasons why a respondent might indicate a relatively low need. If an area is thought to be important, but the individual is well versed in the area, there might be little perceived need.

Likewise, if an area is thought to be unimportant or irrelevant, whether or not the individual has studied the area, there might be little perceived need. Furthermore, although survey research assumes that respondents reply honestly, it is possible that regardless of a respondent's expertise or need, this list of seventeen items was seen as an opportunity to "cast a vote" regarding the importance of certain content areas in technology education.

A rather large number of respondents seemed to recognise no personal learning need that could be met by taking a course or workshop. This is surprising considering that the respondents were professionally involved in education. This view, which was most prevalent in respondents with doctorates, those that have fulfilled job requirements for education, and those near retirement, is contrary to the notion of life-long learning and continued professional development.

Need for Online Technology Education

Two Likert-type questions asked respondents for their general opinion on the need for online technology education. The first question in this area asked: "How much of a need do you think there is for online education in technology education?" The points on the scale were coded with numbers 1 representing "no need" to 5 representing "great need." From the responses to this item, a mean of 3.81 resulted. Sixty-three percent chose the top two levels, and 30% chose "great need," whereas only 1% chose "no need." A similar question asked respondents, "How much of a need is there for online technology education for students in grades K-12?" The mean of 891 responses was 3.49, based on the same 5-point scale. This could indicate further opportunities for online curriculum developers interested in reaching K-12 students.

Relative Appeal of Online and On-Campus Classes. Respondents were asked, "How appealing is each of the following to you?" They were then presented with two items, each with its own 5-point Likert-type scale. The items were "Taking a standard on-campus class" and "Taking an online class." The Likert-type scale headings, coded 1 to 5, ranged from "very unappealing" to "very appealing." On that scale, the average appeal of taking an online class slightly exceeded the average appeal of taking an on-campus class.

Both means were situated between "50/50" and "appealing." Respondents who had previously taken an online course reported greater1 appeal of online classes than did those who had not. Although the reader is cautioned against generalising these survey results to a larger population, it is worth noting that at a minimum,

505 ITEA members (or at least one in seven) found the idea of taking an online course appealing or very appealing.

Educational opportunities can be structured in a variety of ways. It might be that the traditional, three-credit, fifteen-week college course on a fixed calendar is not always the best structure for online educational offerings.

It was suspected that shorter, 1-credit courses might be more attractive due to decreased demands on a student's time. Using a format similar to the previous questionnaire item, respondents were asked to rate the appeal of a 1-credit and a 3-credit class. Within this survey sample, 3-credit courses seemed to be slightly more appealing than 1-credit courses, although the means for both were situated between "50/50" and "Appealing." The flexibility of 1-credit offerings was anticipated to increase appeal, but this was not found to be the case. The greater appeal of 3-credit courses might be due somewhat to tradition but also to the need of teachers to take courses that fulfill their districts or degree's requirements.

Course length is another factor to consider in structuring online courses. Respondents were asked to "indicate the ideal number of weeks you would suggest for a 3 credit online course (between 1 and 15 weeks)." Presenting the mean recommended course length does not adequately describe responses. The top choice was 10 weeks (145 respondents), followed by 15, 6, 8 and 12 weeks. Yet, 194 respondents indicated an ideal time less than six weeks. Universities should consider offering online courses that differ from the length of their traditional courses.

Another logistical factor in course design concerns the course calendar. A questionnaire item asked the following: "Some distance education classes require students to complete the assignments according to a fixed calendar, while others are self-paced. Which would you prefer?" They were then presented three choices: "Fixed calendar," "Self-paced," and "Undecided/ Depends on Content." The number of respondents selecting "Undecided/ Depends on Content" was the greatest, just greater than the number choosing "Self-paced". The third option, "Fixed calendar," was selected by 243 respondents. This does not mean that the preference does not matter, or that these discrepant views cancel each other. Rather, educational providers should be cognizant of the diverse preference of learners.

The final question in this area was an attempt to determine preferences for group or individualised learning structures. When asked to select one of four possibilities, the majority of respondents reported having a preference for "a mixture of independent and group learning." More respondents preferred learning on their own than preferred "learning by interacting with other students". An implication for instructional designers and teachers of online courses is to include a variety of individualised and group learning activities in online classes.

An attempt was made to determine perceived obstacles to taking online courses. Respondents were asked, "For you, what is the biggest obstacle to taking an online course?" The item with the most responses was "no opinion / don't know." This might seem like a response with little semantic impact. However, it parallels many of the comments made in the attached "comments" portion of the instrument. There, several respondents indicated that they had never considered online education before, so they were not aware of obstacles.

Ironically, this may be the most telling data concerning obstacles: "lack of awareness" or no consideration of online education as a viable alternative could be the biggest barrier between many technology education professionals and online educational opportunities. To overcome this obstacle, educational providers would be wise to take on the responsibility of informing the public and their potential clients of the services they offer, paying special attention to describe what it is like to take an online course.

The second and third ranked obstacles were "time requirements" and "I can't find a course I'm interested in or need". For these, and other obstacles, solutions may be possible. Varying course length and timing may successfully overcome some individuals' "time requirements" obstacles, while better publicising online course offerings may help overcome the inability of potential students to locate a course they want.

Other obstacles noted in a comments section tended to be related to: ignorance ("Never given it much thought!"); apathy; personal characteristics ("Need structure of classroom"); computer issues; and questions of quality ("Poor quality of instruction"). However, it should be noted that these are perceived obstacles, and students who enroll in online education may soon overcome a previously perceived obstacle. For example, Wells found that by the midpoint of an online course, "the anxiety surrounding the course requirements and gaining the necessary enabling skills were mitigated."

A survey item asked, "If you were to begin an online college degree program, in which level would you be most interested?" Respondents chose the "master's" level as most appealing, followed by the "doctoral" level and "continuing education credit". As would be expected from the educational level of respondents, relatively little interest was shown in an undergraduate degree.

A second question in this area asked, "If you were to begin an online college degree program, in which area would you be most interested?" A clear favorite here was "Technology Education", over the alternatives of "Educational Administration" and "Curriculum and Instruction".

Most Attractive Aspects on Online Courses. In an open-response question, respondents were asked, "What is the most attractive aspect of taking an online course?" The quantity of responses to this item was high, but the variety of responses was not. By far, the most common responses concerned convenience, which seemed to be partitioned between not having to travel, and the flexibility to work at one's own schedule. This corroborates the work of Thompson who noted that, "Traditionally, distance education has attracted students whose geographic distance from a higher education institution discouraged or prevented enrollment in on-campus classes". However, some respondents indicated that the self-pacing of online education is appealing.

In a parallel item, respondents were asked, "What is the least attractive aspect of taking an online course?" The number of responses to this item was once again great, but the variety was greater than the previous item. The most common response expressed the belief that there would be little human interaction, either with the instructor or with fellow students. This confirms the findings of Schmidt and Gallegos, who surveyed four technology classes at Purdue University to determine issues and concerns of distance learners. Other common responses from the present study concerned low interaction ("No interaction with instructor/classmates"); low quality; time, work, and cost requirements ("Cost / time"); personal characteristics ("Motivation"); computer concerns ("Not being totally comfortable with using the internet"); ignorance and fear ("Unsure of what it is all about"); and availability ("Finding one to take.")

Strategies should be devised to minimise each of these "least attractive" aspects. For example, designers of online instruction might consult newly published standards and principles for online education in their effort to ensure quality. Most significantly, however, is the need to overcome the belief that online courses do not include interpersonal contact.

Ignorance and misconceptions about what an online course entails may pose a problem in analysing the results of this item. Anderson noted that typical students who take their first online course are often unaccustomed to the instructional techniques and mistakenly assume a passive role. It is not feasible to use an online course to overcome such misconceptions if they pose a significant obstacle to enrolling in an online course. Instead, universities and others should educate potential students about what it is like to take an online course. Because there is much variety in both student needs and possible educational offerings, universities should provide sufficient information to potential students that would allow them to wisely choose courses or programs that meet their content needs and learning styles.

Respondents were asked the following question: "If you decided to take an online course or begin an online degree, where would you look to see what is available? Where should universities advertise?" Many stated they had no idea where to look. Others listed ITEA's website and publications. A surprisingly large number of respondents noted that they would look toward local (geographically) sources to find information about online courses. They most commonly included nearby universities, the Web pages of those universities, state organisations affiliated with ITEA, and state departments of education.

The implications for the technology education profession are clear. First, there should be a free, centralised clearinghouse that facilitates easy listings of, and easy searches for, online education in technology education. ITEA is the logical choice within the US for this clearinghouse, though other associations may be more appropriate elsewhere.

A second implication is that universities should use a variety of strategies to disseminate information about online offerings.These include Web-based sources, mailings, organisations, bulletins, and partners. The Web addresses (i.e., URLs) of courses should be submitted to search engines so that keyword searches will find the necessary information about the online offering. Willingness to Teach Online. Respondents were asked, "Would you like to try teaching online (even if that means getting training in online teaching)?" A large number answered, "Yes."

This was higher than had been expected, considering the observation of Williams, Paprock, and Covington. They stated, "When teaching and training professionals are asked to participate in open and/or distance learning projects, many have an underlying resistance to change". Those without prior experience as online students were more likely to answer "Yes" than those who had been online students. Should universities recruit online technology teachers? Should they specifically offer training in "how to teach technology education online"? Should technology teachers provide online K-12 education?

Perceived Online Learning Needs

A variety of views emerged concerning online learning needs. While some people indicated a need for individual courses, others preferred continuing education credits, or entire degree programs. Although the greatest job-related educational need was for continuing education credit, a higher level of interest was expressed for online programs in technology education and at the master's level than in other alternatives. Interest was evident in courses and workshops covering a variety of topics, including activities to teach about technology, new and emerging technologies, technology education curriculum, and using the internet to teach about technology. Teaching methods and student management were also of interest, but more among those who had not yet completed a bachelor's degree. Furthermore, interest was expressed in topics related to the ITEA content standards. Of these areas, the most interest was expressed for "information and communication" and for "technological design." "Medical technologies" and "agricultural and biotechnologies" were of least interest.

Several barriers to meeting online learning needs emerged. Among these were a lack of perception of need, a lack of awareness of online opportunities, a perception that online education is too impersonal, and a perception that online education is of inferior quality. Yet, universities can help overcome some of these barriers if they advertise online offerings that have been designed to ensure both high quality and personal interaction. A number of preconceptions emerged that may not accurately describe online education. For example, a perceived lack of inter-student contact in online courses seems to be contrary to the use of collaborative online strategies and technologies. Other preconceptions that should be scrutinised include a perceived lack of contact with the instructor, a self-paced calendar for an online class, and lower quality of online education compared to traditional education.

Concept of the virtual university

The educational methods accompanying the new technological paradigm allow of a participatory vision of education by promoting asynchronous learning, a new inter-actor relationship and 'lifelong' education. The role played by education software in distance education increased in the period from 1985 to 1995 as it gradually replaced learner-controlled approach instruction or programmed education, in which traditional or audiovisual teaching aids were used. By the year 2000, this development process will have been transformed and broadened, relocating learners and teachers, reconstructing the underpinnings of natural course progression (through the multimedia, for example), channelling reliable and enriched material through the data transmission networks, combining the necessary documentation with lectures, and enabling teachers, researchers and students to exchange information via electronic mail and forums and thus globalizing knowledge.The current information context is characterized by the mass advent of digital solutions, which are drastically changing established realities, and by a major risk of the hegemony of one single language to the detriment of multilingualism and of one single culture to the detriment of plurality, in particular through the very rapid development of the Internet, by the atomized development of the new technologies at different paces in different countries and regions and, finally, by the reduced visibility of non-digitized material for ever-growing communities. And, in parallel, needs are steadily expanding in terms of information and of methods and tools for producing, organizing, disseminating and consulting it. Most of the technical and methodological solutions necessary to this circulation of information, such as the Internet and related standards, have their origin in the scientific community, which must now devote thought to its uses and its inescapable penetration of the world of education and research.

Past experience will have to be analysed in the light of the impact of the digital, particularly on the circulation and transmission of knowledge. Some consider that the concept of the industrialization of education is undergoing profound transformation. Distance education already has a long history of research and achievements, from correspondence courses to systems supported by distance audiovisual aids (which are generally satellite-based). The ICTs are revolutionizing this discipline and should enable it to emerge from arcane debate and the scepticism of educationists, and become a global industry. Whereas the question of the didactic quality of distance education is still the subject of much debate dividing 'traditionalists' and 'specialists', the ICTs are beginning to introduce all the factors of what amounts to an educational revolution, in which the teacher-learner and the learner-learner relationship will change radically. The concepts of 'collaboration' and 'asynchronous education' should gradually become established, more because they reflect the necessities of the evolution of society than for purely educational reasons. This change contains a veritable educational revolution in embryo, in which the traditionally rigid space-time-hierarchy structures will be shattered. The main argument in favour of this change is, of course, economic; but it must be borne in mind that distance education fees are still as high as those charged for traditional education, since the mass economies that will offset an initial outlay higher, in every respect, than that involved in traditional education, have not yet been achieved. This will change radically as the mass application of this technology becomes established - which could be the case after a transition period of several years.There are, of course, still many challenges to be faced:

— the use of various technologies in appropriate proportions and applications,

— the question of the evaluation of learners and teachers,

— the question of intellectual property where educational material is concerned,

— and the major bottleneck: training in the skilled use of these new tools.

Distance education used mainly by education experts, existed before the rapid development of the ICTs, and seems to be resisting technological change. The term might suffer from the fact that a number of education experts are lagging behind in the technological field, but it should retain its status as a term of reference Distance teaching/distance learning/distance-teaching university: characteristic of the audiovisual (televised) stage of distance education and facing a serious threat from the novel contribution of the ICT.

The concept of the virtual university is the most widespread at the present time. It meets traditional universities' need to provide new services and to find new modes of relating to learners. Following are the ingredients of success:

— use of the NICT and a combination of the various technological tools 'in proportion' with a view to radically changing the equation of the cost of education;

— teaching which accompanies the new technological paradigm and makes possible:

— asynchronous learning;

— a new inter-actor relationship;

— continuing education;

— a participatory vision of education; the virtual university is where three areas intersect:

i) the area of possibility;

ii) the technology area;

iii) the teaching area.

ICTs are at the top of the hierarchy, but it must be realized that unless these technologies are applied with the appropriate teaching methods, they will add nothing to education but confusion and mistaken objectives. If, on the other hand, they are mastered, the change of paradigm which they will bring will allow of nothing short of a revolution in teaching, marked primarily by the abandonment of the vertical form of education (vertical transfer of knowledge) in favour of a ring structure, in which the teacher becomes the facilitator of a process which is focused on the learner and on his or her ability to discover knowledge at his or her own pace and in collaboration with other learners and facilitators. Secondly, as the result of an asynchronous mode of operation, this new form of teaching will ease the constraints of space and time. By losing its verticality, learning becomes a process of collaboration and partnership among various groups.

The teaching area is undergoing far-reaching changes. Some recent inputs have been disqualified to a certain extent by technological change, and concepts are currently being revised from the point of view of means and objectives. The major challenge is to devise a new form of teaching which is based on and transcends technological devices without adopting the attitude of a technologist or mythifying technology. The challenge appears to be less contradictory whenever the sociological aspects accompanying the technological revolution are emphasized.

After several years of slow and difficult progress, this discipline has entered a 'push technology' phase, which could come to maturity in less than two years and could give way to a new global market-driven phase, in which market shares will grow significantly in less than five years. We are in a situation similar to that of the Internet in 1992; we are going through a two- to three-year period of transition, which will be followed by a period of tremendous expansion. The following are the three key factors in the 'push technology':

1. the necessary change in teaching methods, and in the student-teacher and student-student relationship in particular;
2. the key ingredients for the change in teaching methods: the pursuit of group interactiveness and proactiveness;
3. determination of the judicious proportion of technological facilities.

The US Science Foundation, which supported the Internet international telecommunications skeleton for many years, suspended its efforts in 1993 to give way to the commercial Internet. After three years of discussion of the importance of allowing the market to take over advanced development, Internet 2 marks the return of the university initiative and, ultimately, it is a qu èstion of organizing the transmission band in order to make distance education possible.

The Europeans have projects which are similar - DANTE in particular - but which are perhaps less geared to building up the infrastructure for distance education.This network of geostationary satellites for digital radio is under construction. As of 1999, it will cover all countries with emergent economies (in Africa, Asia and Central and Latin America), that is to say, a total of over 4 billion people; 10 per cent of the channels will be devoted to education and training, a fact which will make it the most powerful educational instrument in the service of developing countries. The persons responsible for higher education in the countries concerned will be invited to take part in the measures to define and establish appropriate programmes, to assist in the development of appropriate methodologies suited to this new digital technology, and to turn it to good account in all of their fields of competence, particularly that of teacher training.

A number of experiments are being carried out in Latin America. They can be divided into four main categories:

a) several national or regional projects, which are primarily instructional in orientation but which are having great difficulty in keeping abreast of and applying technological advancement (UNA, CREAD, etc.);

b) projects involving considerable investment in technology and a notable strategic capacity for regional establishment, offset by relative weakness regarding the research, sociocultural vision and regional integration complex;

c) several initiatives (in Argentina in particular) which have a notable socio-political vision but which lack the means of having any noteworthy regional impact (Lund, Fasta, Cediproae, etc.) and remain one-off initiatives;

d) the Monterey virtual university project (Mexico), which, despite several shortcomings regarding sociocultural and geopolitical aspects, shows that advances in the field of initial outlay and technological control may prove essential in the regionalization/internationalization of education markets.

The World Bank project for Africa (AVU) is a series of courses of instruction in scientific disciplines offered in the form of university bachelor's and master's degree courses and continuing education units, and is common to many countries. It is placed at the disposal of African countries against payment of a fee. The project uses the ICTs, particularly satellite broadcasting from the United States via INTELSAT 515. The courses are divided into three sub-series - English language, Portuguese language and French language. The World Bank has initially appealed to France, Belgium and Switzerland in the case of the French-language section, and a pilot experiment is under way.

In Europe the first is the Institute for Information Technology in Education, which was set up in Moscow by UNESCO and the Government of the Russian Federation in February 1997 at the conclusion of the International Congress on Education and Informatics. Its main objective is very ambitious - that of elaborating a model of global continuing education for all. By 2000-2003, it should be possible to achieve important objectives through joint action by institutes of higher education at Confederation and Canton level, such as action to improve the quality of the educational experience for students, to transform university teaching and to provide new opportunities of access to higher education (independent of the constraints of space and time), to reduce costs - at least per student, and to provide a better supply of further education.The Open University in the United Kingdom - the historic European 'leader' in the field - should also be borne in mind in this context.

In North America a national university education network is being built up in Canada, which, it is planned, will operate via the Internet and interactive videoconferencing, thus linking the 12 Canadian establishments and gathering all of their programmes together with a view to providing young French speakers with as wide a range of studies in French as possible. The driving force behind this project is the University of Ottawa; this showcase of official bilingualism is situated in the province of Ontario, the home of half of the French speakers outside Quebec, and offers a very rich palette of programmes. Furthermore, the University has been running a distance education network extending throughout the province for the past five years. The UFHQ of Eastern Canada, which are fairly well equipped, have also already offered and received distance courses. The distance factor will no longer be a constraint. The student can take part in education without needing to be present in person at the university. The pedagogical investment for modern distance education is certainly greater than that of the traditional model, whether in terms of initial outlay or the investment connected with delivering the education. There are two factors, however, which will reduce the overall cost in factors of scale:

i. the reduction of needs in terms of area and premises;

ii. the appreciable increase in the size of the virtual class.

The traditionally vertical teacher-student relationship will evolve towards a more horizontal model, in which the teacher becomes a facilitator, expert or colleague and the learner becomes naturally active. In this evolution of roles the group will gain importance as a place for consultation, dialogue and collaboration. Through this mechanism the education is 'received' by the individual in interaction with a group, of which the teachers constitute only one element. Roles are thus completely redefined, and the dynamism of the new roles requires a new student. The internationalization of the education market and the emergence of new entities placed deliberately in the commercial area will intensify competition between educational establishments. In parallel, collaboration and strategic alliances on the part of universities will become imperative as the appropriate response to change.

Rraditional concepts of student assessment based on results will have to be adapted to new methods in which the assessment of the process will gain more importance so that the measuring of assimilated knowledge can be circumvented and factors more sensitive to the equation of the new professional can be integrated: ability to carry out research, to adapt, to communicate, to collaborate, etc. The distinctions drawn between the various types of education will become less important, and the emphasis will be placed on continuing education. As this trend develops, the distinction between 'attendance-oriented' and distance education will become blurred, and the foregoing concepts will also apply to 'local' forms of education.

The advent of the ICTs in the years that lie ahead raises the question of how the teaching profession can prepare for these radical changes. Structurally, distance education is much more demanding as regards teaching ability. The 'new teachers' will have to master this new ICT environment and be mentally prepared for a radical change of role while adding to and updating their knowledge of their special subjects.The new teachers will emerge from the isolation of the classroom and receive considerable logistical support, and it is up to them to be able to co-ordinate and use it: they must have production specialists at their disposal for both audiovisual means and the Web, so that they can achieve high-quality results as regards form and can concentrate on content, i.e. on the educational material.

The realization by university authorities of the need to provide teachers with a set of support functions is a key factor in successful educational production.The production of interactive multimedia as personal learning tools complementing network-based tools seems to be reserved for industry for the time being, and distance universities are slow to apply themselves to this field. Yet there is basically no economic reason for this.

Web-based educational sites are to be observed which have excellent graphic models but response speeds which are too low to serve as an educational tool - a fact which argues in favour of producing interactive CD-ROMs and implementing intranets rapidly. Moreover, the emergence of digital radio (DAB) has made it possible to found new hopes on the mass dissemination of knowledge at low cost and in acceptable conditions.

This technology is particularly suited to developing countries.UNESCO recommends that 'design templates' be created for educational software. Thus, the suppliers of course material will be able to offer programmes in the language of their choice, regardless of the region of the world.

Each producer will be supplied with a compendium of examples of good practice in using NICT-related software. This action should enable the countries of the South to develop good-quality open and distance education rapidly.

The need is growing for measures to defend freedom of access to information in the form of a universal public service intended for the research and education sector in particular. Considerable efforts to put informal literature, reports and theses on line are becoming a matter of priority. The same applies to free software designed according to the ideas of the producer groups; the LINUX operating system and the CDS-ISIS documentary software can be quoted as examples.Multilingualism is an important point in the defence of cultural pluralism as opposed to the monolingualism of information.

Automatic translation tools must be implemented rapidly.The purpose of virtual reference libraries and electronic libraries is to provide all scientists, researchers, teachers, and students with a virtual information site through which they can access all the products necessary to their education, training and research work. The human factor is one of the major factors curbing ICT penetration of higher education.

Before any technological action can be taken, training programmes need to be defined at various levels for various target groups. Plans must be made for training technicians and engineers to back up technology within institutes of education and research, for training teachers, and for training decision-makers. The latter is a sine qua non if the ICT are to enter the scientific world.

It is essential to convince the political and institutional authorities that these technologies are justified as a factor of development and modernity.Various factors must be taken into account when the ICT are being introduced into higher education - an undertaking which is not without risks. The economic imbalance between the countries of the North and those of the South disqualifies the latter.

There are several factors which determine this imbalance:

i) universities do not all have flat-rate connection;

ii) it is paradoxical that the poorest countries should be those where the cost of telecommunications is highest;

iii) computers are still expensive and heavily taxed in those countries, although the states are beginning to pursue incentive policies;

iv) universities are undergoing a reorganization whose contours are still vague and not yet fully understood;

v) there is a risk of cultural uniformization unless diversity - linguistic diversity in particular - is assured;

vi) there is a gap between the academic world and the industrial world;

vii) there is a risk of de-skilling in the case of teachers who cannot or do not want to adapt to the new circumstances;

viii) de facto technological imperialism entails the risk of cultural imperialism if only one part of the world produces material and the other consumes it.

Today universities are in a position to take up the challenge of the new information and communication technologies. To do so they must launch a process of collaborative work in which the least developed countries have an important place. The scientific excellence of the industrialized countries will have to irrigate the poorest countries according to a co-development rationale. The risk of 'infopoverty' is one of the factors curbing development, and it is therefore essential that universities should be the predominant sources of the circulation of knowledge in the service of shared collective intelligence.

Internet Use By Teachers

Todya, majority of teachers use the internet in their effort to find information resources for use in their lessons, and more than one-quarter of all teachers report doing this on a weekly basis or more often. Teachers who use the internet in this way typically have either home or classroom access.

Both home and classroom access are about equally related to use, and teachers who have the combination of both home and classroom access report the most frequent use, with 46% of such teachers reporting weekly or more frequent use. Of course, it is also likely that teachers who want to use the internet may go to some effort to acquire either home or classroom access, but it also may be that the presence of the technology increases utilisation.

Despite these findings, it is also true that even among teachers with both home and classroom internet access, more teachers report only "occasional" use of the internet for lesson preparation than report use on at least a weekly basis. Two additional areas of professional use of the internet by teachers—e-mail with teachers from other schools and publishing on the World Wide Web.

Classroom access to the internet may make a difference in whether they use e-mail for professional purposes: Teachers with internet access both at home and in their classroom were more than three times as likely to e-mail teachers at other schools than teachers who had only home internet access. Also, relatively few teachers have begun posting information, suggestions, opinions, or student work on the World Wide Web.

Just as information-gathering for lesson preparation is the most common use of the internet by teachers, teachers have students use the internet for "research," or information-gathering, more than for any other purpose. In fact, in the past two years, Web searching has become the third most common use of computers by students at school, after word processing and use of CD-ROMs. Web searching even slightly surpasses skills practice by computer drills and learning games in terms of how frequently teachers have students use computers in that way.

Even though a majority of teachers have still not used the internet in their teaching, and even fewer have used it in a major way, there may be many reasons for this – the recent development of internet tools and resources, the rapidity with which technologies are changing, the limited opportunity that teachers have had to see how the internet can be used in their practice, and the rarity of fast and convenient internet access.

Some teachers who have not used the internet may be looking forward to a day when they might. How do teachers see the internet's potential value for them in the near future? Do most teachers see the internet as a valuable or an essential resource in their teaching, as something of limited value, or perhaps something that is not even needed?

We asked teachers about the value of the internet in two respects: the value of a teacher's computer station with electronic mail access; and the value of having World Wide Web access in their classroom. In each case, almost one-half of all teachers saw these resources as "essential" for their teaching and nearly 90% reported that they would consider these resources either valuable or essential. Even among teachers who did not have access to the internet either at home or in their own classroom, one-third regarded the internet as an essential teaching resource.

Clearly, the access that teachers have to the internet as well as their teaching responsibilities affects the likelihood that they will use the internet themselves or with their students and, to some extent, whether they have come to value this resource in their teaching. Certainly teachers have to have access to the internet in order to use it.

In terms of a teacher's own professional internet use, having a modem at home may be almost as important for teachers as having one in their classroom. Teachers with a home modem but no access at school at all have nearly the same Teacher Use score as teachers with an internet connection in their classroom but no modem at home. Moreover, teachers with a home modem but working in a school without internet connectivity still have an average internet Use score that is twice what teachers have who have internet access somewhere in their school but not at home and not in their own classroom.

Teachers with home internet access also have stronger beliefs about the need for internet in their teaching. For student use, teachers with internet access in their own classroom are much more likely to assign students to do work on the internet than where access is limited to locations outside of their own classroom. It does look from these data that home internet access is an advantage for teachers even for stimulating teacher-directed student use. There are also differences in internet use and perceived value between teachers with LAN-based direct high-speed internet connections in their classroom compared to teachers with simple dial-up modem access. These differences are probably understated by our data as indicated in the note above. Teacher Use and Student Research percentages are both somewhat higher for classrooms with LAN-based-direct connectivity than in classrooms with modem connections. It is not, however, just the speed and ease-of-use factors that may be responsible for these differences.

Classrooms with LAN-based-direct connections are more likely to have at least several computers with simultaneous internet connections than classrooms where each connection requires a separate modem. The fact that student internet use is higher in classrooms with LAN-based direct internet connections feeding multiple numbers of computers could be partly due to different subjects being taught in classrooms with more internet connectivity.

To a large degree, teaching students to use computer resources such as the internet remains a specialised province of the "computer teacher" rather than having been integrated into the instructional repertoire of teachers across all subjects. Thus, computer teachers would be expected to have both greater connectivity and to report greater amounts of use.

The teaching profession is generally regarded as having a very flat hierarchy. Each teacher works independently to plan and direct the learning of their own class. This planning occurs with only occasional input from supervisors or colleagues. However, the profession is increasingly recognising that teachers can become better at their craft when many in their profession engage in peer leadership activities—for example, by mentoring less experienced teachers, leading workshops for disseminating new ideas, or writing and publishing for other teachers. Do teachers who become involved in leadership activities of this sort also use the internet more in their professional work? Do they necessarily use the internet more with students in their teaching? Are they more likely to regard it as an essential part of an effective classroom?

Even though software developers have been conscious of the need to make their programs easy for teachers to learn and to use, the power and flexibility of most computer applications inevitably requires teachers master new skills before they can become expert users of computer resources. The new understandings required of teachers include not only technical skills but an understanding of the relevance of the various features and information provided by the software to their own instructional and curricular priorities, as well as pedagogical strategies for using the software in the context of other constraints, such as time limitations and prerequisite student skills.

To accomplish those understandings, many schools provide formal staff development for teachers on computer skills; and some facilitate informal contact among teachers so that the understandings may spread in the normal course of their professional interactions. Nevertheless, one could argue that teachers who were more interested in using the internet participated in this staff development in the first place. To partly control for prior interest and motivation to attend, we looked only among teachers who had the same level of internet access. The "staff development effect," at least as modelled so far, seems to be most clearly present for teachers who have access both at home and in their classroom, or for those without access in either place. In other words, among teachers with the same level of internet access in their classroom, those who have been provided with a computer for their own professional use are more likely to believe classroom internet access to be essential. However, they are no more likely to use the internet in their teaching than are teachers who were not given a computer for themselves. Along with other applications of computers, the internet has been seen by many people as a vehicle for teachers to carry out major changes in how they teach students.

Obviously, having students use the internet is by itself one level of change—a change in the information resources that students examine. But it may also be that the internet enables teachers to follow a whole new approach to teaching based on a different theory of how students attain understanding or new perspectives on what it is important for students to know. Along with word processing, the internet may be the most valuable of the many computer technologies available to teachers and students. In its first few years of existence, the World Wide Web has become one of the most frequently used computer technologies in schools. In addition, hundreds of thousands of teachers have become regular electronic mail users, although that same degree of taken-for-granted access has not yet been provided to many students.

CHAPTER 4

Technology for Teaching and Learning

The way educational technology is developing somewhat resembles the frenetic activities of the White Rabbit in 'Alice in Wonderland'; because it does not seem to know where it is going, any road will do. Educational technology applications though should be driven by our vision of education and training in the 21st century. It is necessary to develop a shared vision of what we want the education and training system to achieve. That vision should take into account the potential of technology, but not be driven solely by what is possible technologically; what it *can* do may not be what we *want* it to do. Those from the business sector are well aware of the global economic changes that are affecting our societies. One of these changes is the need for a much more highly skilled workforce to remain economically competitive and to sustain a prosperous society based on high wages. This is making the training of the existing work-force a high priority, and this training must be continued throughout a person's lifetime. Investment in training is or will become as essential for company survival as capital or plant investment.

It is hard to quantify the need for 'work-force' training, but assuming that a person will need to retrain at least five times in a working lifetime, and that such retraining requires the equivalent of three months full-time learning (probably a gross underestimate), then the capacity of the current education and training market, public and private, needs to be doubled. This is because of increased demand from two sources. The first is from young people continuing into post-secondary education. This demand will continue to increase slightly in most developed countries as more and more young people realise the importance of further education for their future prosperity. However, the major increase in demand will be from all of us in the work-force who need to continue learning if we are to stay employed, and if our employers are to remain economically competitive.

The requirements of this new market for learning are very different from those of the youngsters the system has traditionally served. Much of the learning in the work-force market will be initiated by individuals as part and parcel of their working and leisure lives. It will be informal (i.e. not leading to any formal qualification), self-directed, and piecemeal (broken into small chunks of learning, some as small as a few minutes a day, to some several hours in length). It will be driven as much by short-term needs as by any conscious plan of study. Thus it will not be determined by some master instructor, but by the task at hand. To see just how prevalent this kind of learning is already, just ask yourself how you have learned to use a computer. How much of this was due to formal training, with an instructor, and how much was picked up piecemeal by trial and error, with a bad manual, and help from colleagues? This is not to say that the learning would not have been much more effective if it had been structured and directed all through by a skilled tutor, but what drives such learning is not the control of an instructor but the needs and the motivation of the learner.

Employers however cannot rely entirely on the self-motivation of their employees. This kind of learning, although widespread and surprisingly effective, is not efficient. Management consultants have identified that most companies use less than 10% of the capacity or capabilities of the computer technology in which they have invested. In blunt terms, most employees do not know how to use their machines properly.

As companies increasingly look to higher skill levels from their employees, not just in computer skills, but in the broader skills of verbal and written communication, problem-solving and management, the employers themselves will need to take greater responsibility for making this kind of learning more effective, both to keep valued staff, and to increase productivity.

Traditionally, large companies have done this by establishing their own training centres and programmes; small and medium sized companies have relied more on 'out-sourcing' the training, to private training companies or to the public sector institutions. All of these methods however are labour-intensive, and any increase in such activities will lead to proportional increases in cost, at a time when companies need to be more cost competitive.

While employers will be faced with the need to keep their current work-force highly skilled and up-to-date in the field in which they are working, they will not be able to rely on the public sector to provide, free of charge, the training services they require, for several reasons. In many countries, the public sector institutions still concentrate mainly on pre-service education and training. Furthermore, governments in many developed countries are in serious financial difficulties; they have borrowed too much. Merely servicing the debt is taking away funds that otherwise could be used for public services such as education and training. At the same time, these governments have reached the limit of tax elasticity; the public is unwilling to increase the amount they pay in taxes. In other words, governments are expected to do more with less. Consequently, many public sector institutions are looking on private sector training as a cow to milk, rather than to feed. Lastly, many employers and members of the public are growing increasingly critical about the quality of education being provided through the public sector. There seems to be a mismatch between the skills taught and the requirements of the labour market.

In some ways, this is an unfair criticism, since educational attainment of students in public schools has increased over the last 20 years; the problem is that the demands on the work-force have increased at an even faster rate. For instance, production line workers need greater literacy skills today to deal with written instructions, manuals, etc.; they now need more than just an arm and a leg to operate the production machinery; they need intellectual skills as well. Similarly with greater emphasis on teamwork and worker involvement and motivation, the level of communication and social skills required from managers and supervisors has increased. While a great deal of attention is being paid to the gap between the skills of those entering the workplace and the needs of employers, less attention is being paid to the much wider gap between the skills of those already in the workforce and the demands of the work-place. For instance, the older the worker, the lower the functional literacy level in most developed countries. Another area which needs more attention is the gap between the way educational services are provided, and the needs of employers and working people. Working people are unable or cannot afford to give up jobs or move house to become full-time or even part-time campus-based students again. The most significant development is that many of the new jobs will require a much higher level of skill than the jobs they are replacing, especially in management and resource based industries; people will retain existing jobs only if they are retrained to higher standards; even for the majority of new jobs that will be low-paid and require generally low skill levels, training or retraining will be necessary, especially in basic skills, just in order to keep the job.

Modern learning theory sees learning as an individual quest for meaning and relevance. Once learning moves beyond the recall of facts, principles or correct procedures, and into the area of creativity, problem-solving, analysis, or evaluation (the very skills needed in the work-place in a knowledge-based economy), learners need interpersonal communication, the opportunity to question, challenge and discuss. Learning is as much a social as an individual activity. However, for someone working in a small company, the nearest person with similar interests and expertise may be somewhere on the other side of the country, particularly in leading-edge technologies.

Learners will interact with their desktop or portable workstations in a variety of ways, determined by the nature of the learning task, and their preferred style of learning in the work situation. These preferred styles will vary considerably, both within a single person, depending on the task, and, for the same task, between different individuals. The learning context will need to encompass the following:

— working alone, interacting with learning material (which may be available locally or remotely)

— working collaboratively (and in an equal relationship) with fellow workers at different remote sites, either synchronously or asynchronously: both these modes are likely to be multimedia

— as an 'apprentice' or 'student', working with a more experienced worker, supervisor, or instructor

— as an instructor, supervisor or more experienced colleague for other less experienced colleagues.

The same person may find themselves in each of these roles within a single working day. Learners will also need to be able to work from home, or from a work-site, or while in transit. They will need the following:

— access to information (searching, downloading) from multiple sources in multiple formats;

— selection, storage and re-ordering/re-creation of information;

— direct communication with instructors, colleagues, and other learners;

— incorporation of accessed/re-worked material into work documents;

— sharing and manipulation of information/documents/projects with others.

Learners will need to access, combine, create and transmit audio, video, text, and data as necessary. If we take this as the design requirement, there is then a need to build *systems* that support this form of learning, both for formal and informal learning.

A number of factors are leading many educational institutions to experiment with new information technologies for teaching. There is pressure from governments for greater efficiency, requiring institutions to take more students, while at the same time reducing funding. Another influence is the use by governments of earmarked funds for innovation.

Another factor is the increase in student fees, leading to more and more students becoming part-time, in order to work their way through university. For instance, almost half the students in the universities, and two-thirds of the college students, in British Columbia now are part-time. Also, the trend towards lifelong learning and the need for re-education and training for people already in the workforce is leading to a changing student population, with many more older students, working and with families, returning to post-secondary education. These students need greater flexibility in the provision of learning, to fit it around their already busy and demanding lives. It is not surprising then that many institutions are now turning almost in desperation to multimedia technologies as one possible solution to their increasingly pressing problems.

It is from these often prototype developments that we will see some of the newer models of teaching and learning developing that will meet the needs of the changing adult learning market.For instance, at the University of British Columbia, almost $4 million of its operating grant has been held back over the last two years by the government for an innovation fund for the university. The university has used approximately 50% of this for investment in technology infrastructure, such as fibre optic cabling across the campus, computer networks in buildings, computer labs, networked servers, and video-conferencing facilities, and the remaining 50% for technology applications. Almost all the application money has been used for projects (in each of the 12 faculties) using either World Wide Web or CD-ROM technologies.This has lead to a great deal of innovation across the 50 or so projects that have been funded in this way, and some important lessons have also been learned. Also, some lessons learned in other contexts, such as the use of technology for distance education, have also proved just as relevant for on-campus use of technology. Two-way video-conferencing, using either compressed or full motion television, has been the major new technology used for delivery in many universities and colleges across North America.

One of the most technologically advanced systems of video-conferencing operates between the University of Calgary and the University of Alberta. Video-conferencing has been slow to take off at UBC, but this year one fourth year undergraduate plant sciences course has been delivered in this mode, interestingly with the teaching originating from a community college, the University College of the Fraser Valley, because there were insufficient students at UBC in this specialist area (temperate fruit management) to justify a local teacher. Because of the excellent teaching technique and careful advance preparation of the instructor (Tom Baumann), this has been a very successful course. Video-conferencing has the advantage, from an instructor perspective, of not requiring a radically different approach from regular classroom instruction, and appears quick and easy to mount.

However, unit costs are higher than regular classroom teaching, it does need considerably more preparation time, and students still need to be at a fixed place at a fixed time.The biggest explosion in teaching technology in the last couple of years at UBC has been the World Wide Web (the Web), due to the development of relatively user-friendly hypercard technology such as Mosaic and Netscape. This enables "creators" of materials to store primarily text and graphics on "screens" that provide links to any other "screens" located anywhere on the Web. Thus by merely clicking on a highlighted or coloured section of text, a link can be made to another screen on another computer anywhere in the world.

The main use of the Web to date has been for accessing (and downloading) information. However, a number of institutions have started designing courses using Web technology. For instance, at UBC several courses were designed in 1995 using Web software and local servers for on-campus students.

The first of UBC's distance education courses using Web software is in Continuing Studies, which began offering a course "Mastering Cyberspace", primarily aimed at people who want to use the Web for business purposes. In January 1996 UBC will deliver two Web-based credit courses to students off-campus.

Netscape software lends itself particulalrly to subject areas where there is a need for extensive colour illustration in still graphic form. Thus one of the most successful applications at UBC has been in Geology 202, where the combination of a structured approach to teaching with students able to access UBC-generated data-bases of graphics such as rock slides and rock formations, together with on-line access to other geology

Web sites across the world, has considerably enhanced the flexibility of access for students. At this stage there has been little evaluation of the use of the Web for the direct delivery of distance education courses. The UBC use is primarily that of information transmission, with some self-testing through multiple choice questions and in one case simulations. However, at the time of writing Web software lacks the interactive flexibility of dedicated computer conferencing technology such as CoSy or First Class, although this will be available soon. Protocols also have to be established to ensure that only those who have paid their fees can access either the content or the interactive part of the course. The main constraint of using the Web for direct teaching, once one goes off-campus, is the speed (or rather the slowness) at which pages can be accessed or downloaded. It is one thing to make material available on campus over high-speed networks and high-end modems; it is another to deliver a substantial amount of course materials over public telephone networks, through low-speed modems to the kind of computers that students are likely to have at home. We will be monitoring this aspect quite carefully. It may in many cases be better to provide the materials on a CD-ROM, with only updates being made available via the Web.

There has been a rapid development in recent years of computer-based learning, due to technological developments both in the computers themselves, through faster processing, greater storage capacity and 'embedded' software that enables the integration of graphics, sound and moving visuals from external sources, and in the development of 'peripheral' equipment, such as CD-ROM and videodiscs. This has lead to the development of computer-based multimedia materials (defined as textual data, sound, graphics and moving visuals integrated into a single computer platform). Computers have for a long time been used for drill and practice.

However, the combination of sound output, in the form of a digitized human voice and musical tones, recognition and analysis of human voice input, and feedback of results, has enabled the UBC Music department to apply off-the-shelf commercial software for the teaching of music. Students are asked to recognize either sheet music or tones generated by the computer and match that with their own singing input. Off-the-shelf software, such as Supercard, can also be used for constructing teaching materials, making it much easier for instructors to develop materials for a particular context.

There have been a wide number of projects at UBC in this area. Mark Broudo and colleagues in the Faculty of Medicine have developed teaching materials from scratch to assist students develop skills in the area of cardiovascular measurement, using animation, integrated full video and sound, and text, with multiple choice-type questions providing feedback. The material is structured in modules, with students able to access the material when they need it. Brian Holl, a specialist in turf grass management at UBC, has developed a "virtual" office and laboratory to allow students to diagnose and treat turf disease. Students can click on a number of "tools" in the office and laboratory to access information.

In addition, there is a virtual workbook that allows students to enter their own diagnoses and treatments, which is automatically transmitted to the instructor for checking. The interface also includes links to the

WorldWideWeb, and e-mail and messaging capabilities. One of the more exciting uses of multimedia is the development of expert systems that allow the user to test hypotheses and simulate different conditions and see the outcome.

There are though two large assumptions being made about the use of multimedia. The first is that students will have access to computers, Internet, CD-ROM players, etc.. Student access to computers is increasing, but there is also a need for a clear policy to help students access the necessary technology being used for teaching and learning. While many students now arriving in universities already have their own computers (about 40%), many do not. In any case, there is a need for common standards; multimedia materials require medium- or high-range personal computers and fast networks. These are often not available off-campus or in student's homes.

Again, there are several strategies that can be adopted. Institutions can negotiate leasing arrangements with suppliers, so students can pay a modest rental fee with the option for low-cost purchase at the end of the leasing period. A college can ensure there are ports on campus to allow students to plug in their own computers (much cheaper than providing computer labs).

Capital funds for buildings (and car parks) can be reallocated to support student's off-campus access to courses, thereby reducing the demand for campus facilities. Institutions can form consortia to block-buy long-distance Internet access throughout a province or state for students (the Open Learning Agency in British Columbia has recently negotiated such a deal, allowing students local call access to the Internet and OLA's services from most parts of the province). Governments may even install or buy leased network facilities for educational use, as in New Brunswick, Canada.

A more fundamental issue is the change in cost structures resulting from the development of multimedia courses. In the conventional higher education model, costs have tended to increase with student numbers, or quality drops. In other words, if the student/teacher ratio is kept constant, more teachers are needed. If more teachers are not recruited, class sizes increase, interaction with the teacher drops, and hence quality declines. We have seen over the past 10 years in many countries access to higher education being increased by increasing the student/teacher ratio, or by the hiring of young Teaching Assistants scarcely more than a couple of years ahead of the students they are teaching.

However, the cost structures for pre-prepared multimedia materials are quite different. They cost a good deal of money up-front to create, but once created, they can be used by as many students as necessary with minimal increases in costs. This becomes even more pronounced when the life of the course materials are taken into account.

Original multimedia materials created from scratch have a higher 'starting' or fixed cost than classroom teaching, but after production, the only additional costs are the cost of making and distributing compact discs (assuming that students have their own computer and CD-ROM player). Classroom or lecture hall teaching however increases roughly in proportion to the number of students. In fact, costs increase in steps, depending on the assumption about maximum class or group size before the level of teacher/student interaction, and hence the quality of the teaching, is considered to drop. Thus as student numbers increase, extra sessions or classes have to be opened, and additional teachers or instructors found.

The second assumption is that the quality of interaction with pre-prepared multimedia materials is the same as between individual students and a teacher. This in fact is not the case. Well-designed multimedia materials can both present information and provide a large amount of the interaction and feedback previously provided by teachers. This frees up the time for the teacher then to concentrate just on those areas where person-to-person interaction is critical.

However, computers are not smart enough to anticipate all the questions, misunderstandings, and more importantly, original and creative outputs that students can generate. Thus there is still the need for some form of provision, not only for student/teacher interaction, but even more importantly for interaction amongst students. This can be provided either in the traditional face-to-face small group seminars, or 'on-linei' and at a distance by using e-mail or computer. Basically, with multimedia, the teaching falls into two parts: presentation and interrogation of information, some feedback, and some skills development through the use of interactive, pre-prepared multimedia materials; and counselling, student guidance, knowledge building, argument and creative thinking, hypothesis development and testing, interpersonal skills development, and group work through either on-line or face-to-face group contacts. The aim is to use the most valuable and costly resource - that of the teacher - more efficiently, by allowing teachers to concentrate their time with students on what they can do best, namely encouraging and responding to the great variety of contributions that students make to the learning process.

Many universities are making substantial investments in new technologies for teaching purposes. The increasing ease of use and improved presentational and interactive features of technologies such as the World Wide Web are leading many academics to use technology for teaching for the first time in a significant manner. However, although there has been widespread adoption of new technologies for teaching in the last few years, they have yet to bring about major changes in the way teaching is organised and delivered. Without such changes, though, technology-based teaching will remain a marginalised activity, while at the same time leading to increased unit costs.

Following are the number of different reasons to justify the use of technology for teaching and learning:

i) to improve access to education and training

ii) to improve the quality of learning

iii) to reduce the costs of education

iv) to improve the cost-effectiveness of education.

Different people in different positions tend to place different emphasis on each of these rationales. For instance, what has really set fire to many university professors is the possibility of improving the quality of learning through the use of multimedia. The same professor though who is a startling innovator in the use of the technology for teaching can at the same time violently oppose any suggestion that more students might be served by the institution through using technology: more means worse - or at least more work for faculty. Other professors are fired up by the idea that all the world can access their ideas, their research, their wisdom through the World Wide Web - a passion to widen access to their teaching. This is not always accompanied though by a similar passion to improve the quality of their teaching, as can be witnessed very easily by surfing their Web pages.

Some politicians and business people see technology simply as a replacement for labour, and therefore anticipate that technology when applied properly will reduce the costs of education. Unfortunately, this is to misunderstand the nature of the educational process. While labour costs can be reduced by applying technology, unless done sensitively and carefully it can also lead to a large decline in the quality of learning, which in turn will eventually lead to a less skilled workforce. Lastly others look to technology to improve the cost-effectiveness of education. This is not the same as reducing costs. The argument is that for the same dollar expenditure learning effectiveness can be increased, or more students can be taught to the same standard for the same level of investment. While then technology is unlikely to reduce substantially the costs of education without a parallel loss in quality, the wise use of technology can simultaneously widen access, improve the quality of teaching, and improve the cost-effectiveness of education.

Using technology for teaching can help universities serve the public more cost-effectively, and in particular can prepare students better for a technologically based society. There are also many things that are valuable in education, as in life, that technology cannot do, and we need to recognise that, but that is another topic.

Technology and post-modernist organisations

Before putting forward 12 strategies for institutional change to exploit fully the potential of new technologies for teaching, it is important to understand the relationship between technology and the organisational structure of institutions using technology. Most manufacturing companies producing physical goods have until recently adopted a 'Fordist' organisational model. This is characterised by the production of uniform products ('you can have any colour you like, so long as it's black'), economies of scale (initial setup costs are high, but large volume results in each extra unit having increasingly lower marginal costs), a division of labour (work is broken down into different elements conducted by different classes of worker), hierarchical management (decisions are made at the top, and passed down the line of command), and organisation of people and processes into discrete, large units which themselves are hierarchically managed (e.g. production, payroll, personnel, marketing, sales).

The best examples of this kind of manufacturing organisation and structure in education are the larger, national autonomous open universities in countries such as the United Kingdom, Netherlands, Thailand, Indonesia, India, etc., many of which have over 100,000 students. The nearest examples in Canada are Athabasca University and Tele-Universite, although because of their provincial base they do not really reach the scale and hence 'purity' of the industrial model. However, the rapid increase in the size and scale of 'conventional' universities in Canada, the USA, and many other industrialised countries since the 1960s has led to many elements of the industrial model being found in today's universities, such as division of labour and increasingly large classes. Nevertheless the core activity of teaching in conventional universities has been relatively untouched by the industrial process.

Information technology though has led to the growth of many knowledge-based and service industries which have a very different structure from the industrial or 'Fordist' model.These newer forms of organisation have been labelled as 'post-modern' or 'post-Fordist' in structure and are characterised by the following:

i) heavy dependence on information technologies

ii) customised products and services tailored and adapted to needs of individual clients

iii) creators and developers of new knowledge/new ways of doing things, or transmitters and modifiers of existing information

iv) directly networked to clients: rapid and immediate feedback used to modify products and services

v) rapid development and change: organisations are dynamic and move very fast

vi) often small-scale and specialist; dependent on partnerships and alliances with other organisations with related but different competencies

vii) decentralised, empowered, creative workers, often working in teams

viii) strong leadership characterised by clear but broad vision and objectives, playing an integrating, co-ordinating and facilitating management role

xi) global operations post-modern industry sectors are often chaotic and characterised by new players, new amalgamations and unpredictable emergence of dominant technology-linked organisations

The new technologies will be exploited best by those that establish post-modernist forms of organisation. We have not yet seen any advanced and sustainable form of such an organisation in higher education, but elements are already visible in organisations such as the University of Phoenix's on-line programs, Nova South-Eastern University in Florida, the National Technological University, and the proposed Western Governors' Virtual University in the USA.

Nevertheless, there are certain features of a traditional university that lend themselves to the new post-Fordist environment. First of all, a university is an extremely decentralised organisation. It has a large and highly creative 'core' of staff, faculty, who when they apply themselves are capable of creating new applications software, developing expert systems, and adapting or even inventing new forms of teaching and learning.

Furthermore they have one valuable commodity or quality that is lacking in many dedicated open universities: they have a research capability that enables them to generate new knowledge in a wide range of subject areas that can be assembled and marketed through the use of technology.

Lastly, conventional universities have the advantage of what the marketing people call a strong brand image. There are signs that some conventional universities, with good leadership and a shared vision, and sometimes goaded by strong external pressure from government, are regenerating and restructuring themselves to meet the technological challenge.

Development of Learning Materials

The ease of use or 'transparency' of technologies such as the World Wide Web and video-conferencing makes it much easier than in the past for faculty to develop technology-based learning materials and course delivery. The World Wide Web for instance allows a teacher easily to adapt materials created for lecture or classroom use and present them as attractive colour graphics and text. Once the materials are created as Web pages, it is a simple matter to make them available for off-campus as well as on-campus students. In an increasingly competitive environment, and where technology-based teaching is increasingly open to public inspection, the organisations that will survive, as with any of the other new knowledge-based industries, will be those that provide services that the public values, at a better price and quality than the competition. However, on most Canadian university campuses, amateurism rules in the design and production of educational multimedia.

A feature of many Lone Ranger projects is that technology applications end up as a costly supplement to conventional teaching, merely increasing the students' (and faculty) workload, and the institution's overall unit costs, because teaching with new technologies is rarely accompanied by the substitution of multimedia for face-to-face teaching. For the extra cost of using technology to be justified, it needs to be accompanied by the reorganisation of the teaching process, moving away from fixed, scheduled group instruction to more flexible and individualised modes of learning. Another common problem with the Lone Ranger approach is that often there is never a final product that can be used on a regular basis in a teaching context.

This is because the project drags on, being constantly upgraded or improved, or has to be redesigned as a result of inappropriate technology decisions in the early stages of development. Often the graphics and the interface are poor, compared with commercial games with which students are familiar, and the potential for high quality learner interaction with the multimedia materials is often missed. Products when finished have limited applicability because they are not of high enough standard in terms of graphics and interface, or sufficient in volume, to become a commercial product. In other words, Lone Ranger materials usually lack quality in the final product.

There are several components of quality in technology-based educational materials. The first is the quality of the content, which is where the brand image and the research capability becomes critical. Is this unique or valuable teaching material for which there is a need or demand? This is not usually an issue in most research universities.

However, the second component of quality is the standard of media production. Are the graphics clear? Are the screens easy to read? Is the sound and video easy to hear and see? Are the unique features of each medium (video, audio, text, computing) fully exploited? Is the material well assembled? Is the screen designed in such a way that students intuitively understand the range of activities open to them and how to accomplish them (interface design)?

The third component of quality is instructional design. Are the learning objectives clear? Does the material result in the desired learning outcomes? Does it have the appropriate mix of media to achieve the learning outcomes in the most efficient manner? What is the quality of the interaction between student and learning materials? What is the role of the tutor/ instructor relative to the technology-based learning? Is it well structured? Can the students easily find all the material they need and move around the teaching materials easily?

The fourth is the quality of delivery. Are the materials easy for the student to access? Can learners ask questions or discuss materials with other students? Who gives feedback? What happens if they have technical problems? At what times is help available?

New technologies then are likely to remain marginal, despite high levels of capital investment, and will merely add costs to the system, if we do not at the same time deal with structural changes in our institutions, and in particular if we do not make fundamental changes to the ways we organise teaching.

Vision for teaching and learning

'Visioning' is indeed a technique that allows thos working in an organisation to understand the full rang of possibilities for teaching and learning that technolog can facilitate, and the possible outcomes, acceptable c otherwise, that might result from its implementation. helps people working in an organisation to identify an share certain goals. Even more importantly, a share vision is necessary as a benchmark against which t assess different strategies and actions regarding th development of technology-based teaching. In particular an institution needs to define what balance it wants between face-to-face and technology-based teaching. An institution could for very good reasons decide not to go down the technology-based teaching route and place special emphasis on face-to-face and personalised teaching.

It is likely though to be a very elite and high cost institution. Alternatively, an institution might wish to vary within its structure the degree of dependency on technology-based teaching, giving more emphasis for instance to face-to-face teaching at the graduate level, and more to technology-based teaching at the undergraduate level. Lastly, other institutions may make a clear decision to emphasise technology-based learning throughout all its teaching.

Another issue that should be covered in a vision statement is the extent to which an organisation sees itself operating on a local, regional, national, or international basis, and the implications of that for courses offered and student services. This is important because technology-based teaching does not respect political or geographical boundaries. For instance, regional colleges may need to redefine their role if students are capable of accessing the college's standard courses from other, perhaps more prestigious institutions, anywhere in the world.

The vision included several detailed scenarios of teaching and learning for different types of learners. There were several key features in the vision:

— a mix of teaching models, from programs delivered entirely in a face-to-face mode to courses available entirely at a distance; it was envisaged though that most students would take a mix of face-to-face and technology-based teaching over the life of a full degree program;

— an increase in the provision of technology-based non-credit, certificate and diploma programs, aimed particularly at mature students;

— learning materials developed as discrete modules for multiple uses, i.e. the same CD-ROM might be used for on-campus and distance undergraduate students, as part of a certificate program, as continuing professional education for individuals, and as a stand-alone CD-ROM for employers/companies;

— more flexible admission and access, particularly for mature students, through the use of technology-based learning, allowing more students to be admitted to the university.

One of the main challenges of making technology-based teaching a core function is to extend its implementation from a relatively small number of enthusiasts and early adopters to the main body of the teaching force. This means introducing a strategy for inclusion, to ensure that all faculty are encouraged and supported in their use of technology for teaching. Because initially the funding for innovation was held back from general operating grant, the university applied the same principle as the government: faculties' operating budgets were reduced proportionally, then they were encouraged to put forward ideas as to how to spend 'their' proportion of the operating grant held back by the university for applications of technology. Thus instead of grants being awarded on a competitive basis across the university, each Dean made an assessment of the priority for funding for particular projects within his or her own faculty.

This had two consequences. Innovation grants had relatively weak criteria, in terms of conditions required;

and secondly the money was spread right across the university roughly in proportion to the size of each faculty or department. This meant that between 1994 and the present, a relatively large number of academics in every faculty has had some hands-on experience of developing technology-based materials.

Many universities have old buildings without adequate conduits for wiring, or asbestos fillings within walls that need to be removed before modern cabling can be installed. Many faculty and staff will not have a computer or know how to use one. Servers will need to be installed within each department, and networked to other servers on campus. Internet connections with the outside world will need to be established, and ports and other communications facilities installed to enable students in residences or off-campus to access the main university campus, or satellite campuses and other institutions to be linked. While such a technology infrastructure strategy is absolutely essential, unfortunately it is often the first - and sometimes the only - strategy adopted by universities: build it and they will come. However the technology infrastructure plan should be driven by, not lead, the university's overall vision and strategy for its teaching.

There are in fact three levels of support required to fully exploit technology. The most obvious is the technical support, the people who make the networks operate and service the computers and telecommunications. At the second level are media production and services, those who produce educational products or supply educational technology services, such as interface designers, graphics designers, video-conferencing managers, or graduate students who do

HTML mark-up. At the third level are those that provide educational services, such as instructional design, faculty development, project management, and evaluation. The major part of physical infrastructure, such as networks and major equipment purchases, is usually funded from capital budgets, and as such is less likely to compete for funds that impact directly on teaching, such as general operating budget. The cost of the human support though does compete directly with funds for teaching and research.

Furthermore the human cost of infrastructure support is recurrent, i.e. has to be found each year, whereas physical infrastructure is often seen as a once-only investment, although rapid advances in technology and hence the need continually to replace or update networks and equipment make this a dangerous assumption. As a consequence, the human support side is often underfunded. Probably the most consistent complaint across universities from those responsible for technology applications is the inadequacy of resources for technical support. Even so, the further down the chain, from technological support to educational support, the more difficult it becomes to secure adequate resources. If the network crashes, its impact is obvious; the value of an instructional designer is much harder to sell when funds are tight.

IBM survey found 60% of USA university and college students had convenient computer access. At UBC, 70% of all undergraduates already have internet accounts. However, while access continues to grow, it is strongly related to income, gender and profession. Many of those that do have computers have machines that are not suitable for multimedia or internet access. There is also a chicken and egg issue here. If students are not required to have a computer for their studies, they are less likely to purchase one. If students who are thinking of purchasing a computer are not given clear specifications as to what is needed, they are more likely to purchase a less powerful model. Nevertheless, it would be a reasonable assumption to assume that within five years, at least in North America, most university students, both on and off campus, will have convenient access to a computer and internet access. Universities though will need to put in place strategies to help students acquire the most appropriate kind of computer for their studies, and to help those students who do not have and cannot afford to purchase their own computer and network access.

There are several strategies that can be used to provide support for student access to computers. One is to provide computer labs on campus for students. Once again this is a useful start-up strategy, but in the long run it becomes unsustainable as the primary source of student support.

There are several drawbacks to relying on computer labs for access. The first is that as the need to use computers for learning increases, either capital investment costs get out of control, or students' lining up for access reaches unacceptable levels. Secondly, given the rate of technological change, computers in labs quickly get out of date. More importantly, it requires students to access learning from a specific place, often at a specific time, if they have to book, thus removing one of the main advantages of using technology, its flexibility. There will always be a need for specialist computer labs, for those subject areas requiring exceptionally high end or specialised machines and software. There will also always be a need for on-campus access through plug-in ports or drop-in labs for casual use. However, in the long run the most flexible and most cost-effective approach is to encourage students to provide their own computers and internet access. Such a policy though cannot be implemented unless it is clear that students will need a computer, and that means ensuring that there are sufficient courses designed to exploit fully the instructional benefits of using a computer. Will access to a computer be compulsory for certain courses? Will a whole program require computer access? Which courses or programs should be the first to implement such a policy? Will there be common technical standards for computers for all the courses in a program requiring the use of a computer? Students will need answers to these questions. This requires each department to develop a clear strategy for the use (or deliberate non-use) of computers, and this strategy needs to be clearly communicated to potential students. These departmental strategies need to be co-ordinated at a faculty and institutional level, so that students do not coninually have to change machines, operating systems, internet service providers, etc.

Sonoma State University, California, spent two and a half years preparing for the implementation of a policy requiring all freshmen students to have a computer. They made sure that there were sufficient courses developed in a way that exploited the use of a computer, and therefore made it essential and valuable to use one. This required a major investment in faculty development. Sonoma State put in a place a whole range of strategies to help students who could not afford a computer: a work-on-campus scheme whereby students could get a computer then work to pay it off; relatively few students at Sonoma qualified for some form of supplementary State or federal grant that would enable them to purchase a computer, as those eligible for a grant were usually already 'maxed-out,' i.e. were already receiving maximum allowable benefit, so for these students, there was a low-cost rental scheme and for some free loans of computers from a pool donated by IBM and Apple. There was an additional 'technology fee' imposed on all students. This was used to provide technical help support for students, improving the local area network, providing docking ports for portables, and making available easy access to public computers in public places on campus. Students themselves play a large role in managing this fund and in approving the level of the fee.

Sonoma State found that there was very high compliance for its policy of requiring all its freshman students to have a computer, it was well received by parents and by employers, who praised the university for making higher education more relevant, and also most students seemed to be pleased with the policy. The important point here is that it was a total strategy. Implementing only part of it - such as a technology fee when many students clearly don't need to use a computer for their studies - can lead to considerable student and faculty resistance. Other strategies to increase the accessibility of computers and networks for learners are the development of government-funded educational networks, through contract leasing or bulk buying of telecommunications services, tax breaks for students on computer purchase, and the development of local community learning centres equipped with advanced technologies.

Lastly, while technology may open up access to some and deny it to others, computer ownership is not the main obstacle to university access at the University of

British Columbia. Many more potential students are denied access by restrictive grade point average entrance requirements, arbitrary prerequisites, residency or attendance requirements, and barriers to credit transfer from other institutions. If a primary purpose of introducing technology-based learning is to increase access, these admission policy issues need to be addressed as well.

New teaching models

The newer technologies are quite flexible in that they can be used in a variety of different ways for teaching. Technologies can be used to replicate traditional forms of teaching; at the same time, they can be used in quite new and different ways, depending on the imagination, skills and resources available to the teacher or learner. Nevertheless, despite this variability, certain trends in the use of technology are evident. It appears that some technologies lend themselves more easily to certain approaches to teaching and learning, while other technologies lend themselves to others. There is no super technology that can meet all teaching and learning requirements, so technologies need to be mixed and matched to the educational purpose. Thus we find that instructional television and video-conferencing (one- or two-way television from one site to a class in another site) and certain applications of the World Wide Web (for instance, where information is posted for students to read) tend to be used primarily for information transmission in a didactic style, very close to the classroom lecture model. Other technologies, such as computer mediated communication using software such as Soft Arc's First Class, Simon Fraser University's

Virtual-U, and Netscape's Hypernews, allow for more collaborative learning models. These technologies encourage or require a high level of discussion and participation by the learner, and very much resemble the seminar model of classroom teaching.

Although CD-ROM technology is often used merely to replicate a book (i.e. a didactic style), but with better graphics, animation, audio and video, a number of applications that more fully exploit the technology are emerging. Thus CD-ROMs are increasingly being used to simulate human interaction (for language teaching), for representing expert systems, such as forestry management, and for problem-solving approaches based on scientific methodology, through for example the use of virtual laboratories.

These approaches to learning enable students to apply their learning to para-realistic situations, to test their own ideas and use their own experience, and as a result to make and test decisions drawing on their previous learning, or even learning facts and principles during the process of decision-making. The Web is a particularly interesting technology in the way that it is evolving. It has the ability to combine all these various approaches to learning. For instance, WebCT, designed at the University of British Columbia by Murray Goldberg, is a Web authoring system that combines didactive and collaborative learning tools, as well as a student learning management system, allowing subject experts without any specialist computer skills to construct their own courses.

The limitation of the Web at the moment is bandwidth and the power of desktop machines, which make it difficult or impossible to run the more powerful applications needed for expert systems, complex simulations and problem solving. However this will change quite rapidly. These technologies enable more powerful applications of such teaching methods in more flexible and accessible forms for students, with also the potential for economies of scale. Furthermore, what all these technologies have in common is that, when well designed, they enable learners, irrespective of the subject matter, to develop skills of information navigation, acquisition, and analysis, application of knowledge to new situations, new knowledge creation, and decision-making, all skills essential for survival in an information society. In terms of change strategies, these new approaches need to be tested and developed not just in a narrow setting of a particular class or course, but in a system of teaching as a whole, where appropriate replacing, not adding to, conventional teaching methods. Thus technology-based teaching needs to be built into the mainstream teaching, and not offered as peripheral or optional learning for students.

Faculty agreements and training

Teaching with technology is not something that can easily be picked up along the way, as something to be done off the side of the desk while engaged in more important or time-consuming activities such as research. The most common form of training given to faculty is to show them how to use the technology. This though is starting at the wrong place. Many faculty need to understand *why* it is important to use technology for teaching in the first place. It has to be related to the changing environment in which universities find themselves, and in particular to the changing needs of learners.

Some basic understanding of the teaching and learning process, and in particular the different kinds of teaching approaches, and the goals they are meant to achieve, need to be understood. The faculty need to understand the different roles that technology can play in teaching, and how this alters the way that teaching needs to be organised. Only then does it make much sense to train faculty in how to use a particular piece of technology. While this sequence may be logical, it is unlikely to be the most effective way to help faculty develop skills in using technology; 'show and tell' and hands-on experience are most likely to lead to this full range of understanding. Nevertheless all four aspects need to be deliberately targeted in faculty development.

University teaching is probably the last craft- or guild-based profession. However, the changing nature and variety of learners, the growing complexity and volume of knowledge, and the impact of technology on teaching now really require that university teachers should have formal training and qualifications in instructional methods. This should eventually become a condition for tenure. Even more fundamental than faculty training is the need to change the reward system for faculty. While many universities have statements that equate teaching with research for tenure and promotion, the reality in most research universities is quite different: the only criterion that really matters is research. Thus there is no point in pouring millions of dollars into infrastructure and computers and multimedia unless the faculty reward system is changed.

Teaching ability must become in practice at least equal to research for promotion and tenure. The good news though is that technology-based teaching is usually more public, more observable, and hence more easily evaluated than conventional classroom methods. Furthermore, multimedia technologies provide an excellent means to convert research knowledge directly into teaching and into promotional material for the research itself. Another way to reward faculty is to ensure that revenues generated by the use of technology by a department flow back into that department, and do not get swallowed by the central bureaucracy. Innovative mechanisms need to be developed for faculty (and other creative staff) to share in rights and royalties from the development of generic educational software and learning materials. Lastly the very sensitive issue of faculty agreements needs to be addressed. There are short-term advantages in leaving things loose, but technological innovation will become unsustainable as faculty become more experienced, suffer from increased workloads, and find that they are still unrewarded.

Project management

New technologies require new applications, a great deal is already known about the *process* of producing high quality, cost-effective multimedia learning materials. This knowledge has been developed both in the large autonomous distance teaching universities, and also in private sector multimedia companies in areas such as advertising and film and television making. This means establishing each course or teaching module as a project, with the following elements:

— a fully costed proposal, which identifies

— the number and type of learners to be targeted (and in particular their likely access to technology),

— clear definition of teaching objectives,

— choice of technologies,

— a carefully estimated budget allocation (including staff time, copyright clearance, use of 'fixed' media production resources, such as video-compression, as well as actual cash),

— a team approach, involving any combination of the following:

i) subject experts/faculty,

ii) project manager,

iii) instructional designer,

iv) graphics designer,

v) computer interface designer,

vi) text editor,

vii) internet specialist,

viii) media producer,

depending on the design of the project,

— an unambiguous definition of intellectual property rights and a clear agreement on revenue sharing,

— a plan for integration with or substitution for face-to-face teaching,

— a production schedule with clearly defined 'milestones' or deadlines, and a targeted start date,

— an agreed process for evaluation and course revision and maintenance,

— a defined length of project before redesign or withdrawal of the course.

New organisational structures

In the 1960s and 70s many universities invested in expensive, centrally managed television studios. More recently universities have established large central computing organisations. Too often these central services have had little impact on the core teaching activities of an institution, partly because faculties have felt that they do not control them. Such units are often subjected to attempts by Deans to break them up and reallocate their funding back to the faculties. Although often dependent on centrally provided networks, new technologies such as the Web are more decentralised. The power is often on the desktop. This provides considerable empowerment for the individual faculty member.

High quality educational multimedia requires a range of specialist skills that go beyond the capability of any single individual. Furthermore the appearance of decentralisation in the new technologies is deceptive. They depend on agreed standards and networks for communication and inter-operation, and they depend on human and technical support infrastructures that require policy making across the university. The initial strategy at UBC in responding to the challenge of the Innovation Fund was not to centralise all the new technology support services into an existing unit such as Computers and Communications or Media Services, nor to set up a large New Media Centre, as many other universities have done, but to establish a very small co-ordinating unit, originally called the Media Resources Network and later the Centre for Educational Technology. This had a project director, a multimedia graphics designer, an interface designer, and later a part-time secretary. These provided services that could be called on by faculty to help them if they wished. This now means that UBC has several small-sized organisational units with somewhat linked activities: Media Services, which provides printing, photography, audio and video production and video-conferencing facilities, the Centre for Educational Technology, the Distance Education and Technology unit, which has project managers, instructional designers and more recently an internet specialist, the Centre for Faculty Development and Instructional Services, and Computer and Communications, which provides network services across campuses and a somewhat decentralised computing support service for faculties.

Health Sciences has its own media services unit and educational support units. Each of the directors of these units have different reporting relationships. Lastly, as well as individual faculty members or departments hiring graduate assistants to provide educational technology support, at least one Faculty has now appointed its own Director of Information Technology and Instructional Support. This sounds like a recipe for chaos, but it works surprisingly well. For large projects, teams can be called together from across the various groups. Thus a project to put the whole of an introductory microbiology program on to CD-ROM and the Web has funding from the Faculty of Science, the Teaching and Learning Enhancement Fund, and the Distance Education fund, faculty and a project manager from Science, an instructional developer from Health Sciences, graphics and interface design from CET, media production from Media Services, and an internet specialist from Distance Education and Technology.

A major study of managing technology for teaching and administration in Australian higher universities classified universities into three different groups: old, divisional and new. The study argued that while centralisation of services is appropriate in a new institution with a major commitment to make IT a centre of its vision and strategy, this is less likely to be appropriate for large, well-established 'divisional' universities with a strong Faculty structure.

New technologies are resulting in global competition for universities. Already three Canadian universities are vigorously promoting and offering distance MBA's in British Columbia. In 1995 43% of all Masters in Education awarded to British Columbia teachers were from institutions in the USA. This competition is going to increase and will be impossible to regulate.

The need for systematic research and evaluation into the use of new technologies should be obvious. However it is important that the right kind of research should be done. The wrong kind of research is to compare the learning effectiveness of technology-based teaching with the learning effectiveness of classroom based teaching, *using the classroom based model as the baseline.* Many hundreds of thousands of such comparative studies have been made in the past, and the usual result when the comparisons have been done using sound research methodology is that there is no significant difference.

As long ago as 1974, Wilbur Schramm pointed to the flaw in this kind of approach: technologies allow the achievement of *new* or different learning outcomes to those of the classroom lecture method, but if the classroom 'event' is the base, then the new learning outcomes that could be achieved are not usually measured. For instance, if a lecture is used primarily for transmitting information, but a CD-ROM is used for applying that knowledge to solving a problem, then the measure of success for the CD-ROM has to be different from the classroom lecture. The aim then should be to measure the success or otherwise of new technologies in extending the range of learning skills, *as well as* content acquisition. Even more important than research into learning outcomes is research into learners' response to using technologies, and in particular what learners and teachers believe may be lost or gained in using such approaches to learning. These results are likely to vary considerably from individual to individual, so it is important to see whether there are groups or types of learners who benefit more than others from technology-based teaching. This kind of research should also help identify the critical aspects of face-to-face teaching, which are likely to be as much social as instructional.

Technology Use in Schools and Classrooms

Modern technologies have transformed many aspects of life, including how we communicate, how we spend our free time, and especially how we work. As life and workplace demands have changed as a result of this "technological revolution," so have conceptions of the skills and knowledge children will need to become successful adults and the relevant educational experiences they should encounter while attending school. As a result, technology, specifically in the form of computers and the internet, has become a major focus of education policy and reform in recent years. National, state, and local initiatives have provided schools with computer hardware and software, allowed schools and classrooms to connect to the internet, and supported technology-focused professional opportunities for teachers. As the numbers of computers and access to the internet in schools have grown, so have the number of questions being asked about the extent to which these technologies are being used in schools and classrooms and for what purposes. Over the past 20 years, education technology has been a major focus of reform and policy at the federal level, as well as at state and local levels. Such initiatives have been guided by the goals of increasing the availability of computers in classrooms and schools, assisting schools with internet access, and providing resources and guidance for teacher training and the integration of technology into the curriculum. The availability of computers and the internet has increased significantly in the nation's schools and classrooms. This increase has been coupled with initiatives aimed toward understanding how best to use technology to improve teaching and learning and training educators to use technology effectively.Existing research on education technology includes a small number of national studies that describe teachers' use of technology, as well as their training to use these tools. Specifically, this research suggests that most current and past uses of education technology have typically supported traditional notions of teaching and learning. For example, in the early 1980s, students most often used computers for drill and practice. Typically, drill-and practice software consists of sequences of worksheet-style questions that automatically adjust their difficulty to match individual students' responses. Also, in the early 1980s, teachers typically used computers to teach students programming skills. They rarely used computers for content-related instruction; students were more likely to learn about how to use computers at school than they were to use computers to learn about mathematics or social studies.

In the early 1990s, the practice of using computers for programming had declined considerably and an emphasis on using computers as a tool for learning content had emerged. However, the primary use of computers remained drill and practice in elementary schools in the early 1990s. In high schools, it was classes on computer education, and middle schools provided a combination of drill and practice and computer education. Finally, as the decade of the 1990s progressed, school computer use had shifted to some degree to reflect a greater emphasis on problem solving and in-depth learning and less emphasis on drill and practice and basic skills. Fulton (1997) found that 25 percent of the 1996 high school graduates who participated in the Scholastic Assessment Test (SAT) program reported having used computers for solving math problems, processing data, or computer programming. Approximately 10 percent had used computers to solve problems in natural science. Using a nationally representative sample of teachers, the Teaching, Learning, and Computing Study found that CD-ROM reference and surfing the internet were more likely to be assigned as classroom activities than games and traditional drill-and-practice applications. However, many of these newer uses have been limited to a small proportion of teachers and students.

Teachers are in fact using computers or the internet generally more frequently to complete a number of instruction-related tasks than to augment instruction itself. For example, they may use these technologies to help prepare for classroom instruction (e.g., to access research on best practices, download information to present in class) or to complete administrative tasks (e.g., to record and calculate grades).

In US, two-thirds of all teachers used the internet in their effort to find information for use in their lessons, and about one-third reported doing so on at least a weekly basis. In addition, teachers may also use technology to communicate with parents or students about students' performance, assignments, or special events. They may also use technology to communicate with other members of their profession to share ideas or strategies for presenting content or helping students who are struggling with the content. As the brief history of technology use for learning suggests, the way educators teach and students learn has not changed dramatically over the past two decades. The research on teacher change and instructional reform in general indicates that such changes in teacher practice are often slow, minimal, or even nonexistent. A number of factors contribute to the success or failure of instructional reforms. One important factor the literature has identified is that teachers do not always have opportunities to learn about and practice instructional reforms.

In the area of technology, teachers may have learned about how to use computers and adapt their teaching from a variety of sources—teacher preparation programs (for prospective teachers), professional development activities (for practising teachers), and informal learning opportunities such as assistance from classmates, colleagues, or students. Professional development research suggests that teachers' opportunities to learn about education technology during traditional professional development activities are often lacking. Often described as an important vehicle for school reform, professional development activities in general have been widely criticised for being relatively ineffective.

Specifically, they have been described as short term, devoid of continuity due to inadequate follow-up and the lack of ongoing feedback from experts, isolated from the participants' classroom and school contexts, and characterised by too few opportunities to learn by doing and reflecting with colleagues. In fact, while a majority of teachers participate in such activities, a small percentage of teachers report feeling very well prepared to integrate technology into instruction. Teacher preparation programs have received similar criticisms.

Traditional programs for prospective teachers have been described as fragmented, superficial, and unconnected to real classroom experiences (National Commission on Teaching and America's Future [NCTAF]. With respect to education technology, some observers have claimed that prospective teachers are not getting the training they need to successfully integrate technology into classroom instruction. For example, some researchers have reported that most students training to become teachers do not routinely use technology while in the field and do not work under supervising teachers who can advise them on using technology in the classroom.

Additionally, about half of the technology training that prospective teachers get in the classroom is delivered as part of other classes (i.e., methods and curriculum classes), and the other half is provided in the form of stand-alone technology classes. Furthermore, most teacher-preparation programs provided by schools, colleges, and departments of education do not have written, funded, regularly updated technology plans.Informal learning opportunities, in addition to these formal learning opportunities, may also provide teachers with assistance using technology. Peer collaboration, in particular, has been heralded by many teachers, researchers, and policymakers as essential for teachers' continuous learning. Teachers may benefit when they learn about technology from one another and provide one another with motivation to continue working with this resource.

In recent years, policymakers have recognised that teachers and administrators need resources and organisational capacity to implement instructional reforms. For example, teachers' ability and willingness to use computers and the internet may depend, to some extent, on the schools and classrooms in which they work. Specifically, certain characteristics of classrooms and schools, such as equipment, time, technical assistance, and leadership, may act as either barriers to or facilitators of technology use.

On a most basic level, teachers may be more likely to integrate computers and the internet into classroom instruction if they have access to adequate equipment and connections. As the number of computers in schools has grown, so has the availability of the internet in schools and classrooms. Between 1994 and 1998, internet availability among public schools increased from 35 to 95 percent. However, availability is not the same as use.

Although the presence of computers and the internet has grown sharply in recent years, much of the technology equipment currently in schools and classrooms is from an earlier generation of technology—computers with less processing power, less storage capability, and limited capacity for being linked together electronically. Using data from 1998, Anderson and Ronnkvist have concluded that although computing capacity for instruction has improved substantially over the past several years, there are a number of "major deficiencies". For example, they found that most of the computers in schools do not have the capability to run a large variety of multimedia software and are also limited in how they can access graphical information on the internet.

The nation's schools have been increasingly challenged by policy initiatives "to do better, and to do differently", pushing teachers to change the way they teach. At the same time, teachers face many other challenges, including rapidly increasing technological changes and a greater diversity in the classroom. With regard to technology, there is often little time in teachers' schedules to become familiar with hardware and software or to learn to integrate the new technology into their lesson plans. Lack of time to become acquainted with technology and learn to use it has been identified as the greatest obstacle to the effective use of education technology. A full-time computer coordinator, for example, may assist teachers with using computer software and hardware or adapting their teaching practice to include computer or internet use. However, according to one study, less than 5 percent of all schools have such a staff member. Furthermore, where they are present, computer coordinators typically spend a significant amount of time teaching students, and much less time assisting teachers.

Principal leadership has been described as one of the most important factors affecting the effective use of technology in classrooms. Principals who exhibit leadership are instrumental in modelling the use of technology in classrooms. They understand how it can support best practices in instruction and assessment and provide teachers with guidance for its use. Principals may also participate actively in professional development activities related to education technology and provide teachers with opportunities to learn how to use these resources. For some teachers, lack of principal leadership may prove to be a barrier to their effective use of technology.

Following are the results of the 1999 Fast Response Survey System (FRSS) survey on teacher use of technology. Specifically, three types of technology use are discussed: (1) preparation and administration, (2) classroom instruction, and (3) communication. Included is information that relates technology use to school and teacher characteristics. National Assessment of Educational Progress (NAEP) asked both teachers and students about computer use over the past four administrations of the surveys. The surveys were administered in 1992, 1996, and 1998. In 1998, teachers of grades 4 and 8 were asked the extent to which they assigned students to use computers for a number of instructional purposes, including: to practice spelling, punctuation, and grammar, to write drafts, to read stories, and to use software for reading instruction. Teachers of fourth- and eighth-grade students reported that their students used computers for writing drafts most frequently.

In 1999, the 99 percent of public school teachers who reported computer availability in school indicated that they used computers or the internet at school to accomplish a number of preparatory and administrative tasks. Overall, 78 percent of public school teachers used computers or the internet at school to create instructional materials, and 59 percent of teachers reported using computers or the internet at school to gather information for planning lessons.

Public school teachers also used computers or the internet at school for administrative record keeping, accessing research and best practices for teaching, preparing multimedia presentations for class, and accessing model lesson plans. In addition to using computers or the internet at school for preparatory and administrative tasks, the 82 percent of teachers with computers available at home also used these technologies at home for such purposes. School teachers used computers or the internet at home to create instructional materials, to gather information, as well as for administrative record keeping, accessing research and best practices for teaching, preparing multimedia presentations for class, and accessing model lesson plans.

Teachers' use of technology for preparatory and administrative purposes varied by a number of school and teacher characteristics. For example, among teachers with computers available in their schools, secondary teachers were more likely than elementary teachers to use computers or the internet at school for administrative record keeping, and they were also more likely to do this at home than elementary teachers.

Moreover, teachers in schools with the fewest students enrolled were more likely than teachers in schools with the highest enrolments to use these technologies at school to gather information for planning lessons. On the other hand, teachers in schools enrolling more students were generally more likely to use computers or the internet at school for administrative record keeping and at home for this task.

In addition to instructional level and enrolment size, there were a number of differences by school minority enrolment in the percent of teachers reporting that they used computers or the internet for preparatory and administrative tasks. For example, teachers in schools with lower minority enrolments were more likely than teachers in schools with the highest minority enrolments to gather information for lesson plans using these technologies at school.

Teachers in schools with fewer minority students were also generally more likely than those in schools with the highest minority enrolments to use computers or the internet at school for administrative record keeping and creating instructional materials.

Finally, teachers in schools with the lowest minority enrolments were more likely than those with the highest minority enrolments to use computers or the internet at school for preparing multimedia presentations.

As is the case with teacher reports from schools with varying minority enrolments, teacher reports of whether they used computers or the internet for various preparatory and administrative tasks varied by poverty concentration of the school, as measured by the proportion of students eligible for free or reduced-price lunch. For example, teachers in schools with the lowest poverty concentrations were more likely to use computers or the internet at school to create instructional materials than teachers in schools with the highest poverty concentrations. In addition, teachers in schools with lower poverty concentrations were generally more likely than teachers in schools with the highest poverty concentrations to use these technologies at school to gather information for planning lessons.

Teachers with varying years of teaching experience differed with respect to whether they used computers or the internet to conduct a number of preparatory and administrative tasks. For example, teachers with the fewest years of teaching experience were more likely than teachers with the most experience to use these technologies at home to gather information for planning lessons and to create instructional materials. Teachers with 4 to 9 years of experience were more likely to use computers or the internet at school to access research and best practices examples than those with 20 or more years of experience.

Finally, teachers with less than 10 years of teaching experience were generally more likely to use these technologies at school to access model lesson plans than those with 10 to 19 years of experience and at home to conduct this task

Public school teachers with computers available in their schools used computers or the internet to communicate with colleagues most frequently, compared to communication with parents, posting homework or assignments, and communication with students.

Teachers' use of technology for communicative purposes varied by a number of school and teacher characteristics. For example, elementary teachers were more likely than secondary teachers to use computers or the internet at home to communicate with parents. On the other hand, secondary teachers were more likely than elementary teachers to use these technologies at school to communicate with students.

Furthermore, teachers in schools with medium-sized enrolments were more likely than teachers in schools with small enrolments to report that they used computers or the internet at home to communicate with colleagues. Teachers in schools with large enrolments were also more likely to use these technologies at school to post homework or assignments.

Teachers' use of computers or the internet for communicative purposes also varied by minority enrolment of the school. Teachers in schools with lower minority enrolments were generally more likely than teachers in the highest minority schools to use these technologies at school to communicate with colleagues.

Similarly, teachers in schools with lower minority enrolments were also more likely to use computers or the internet at school to communicate with parents than teachers in schools with the highest minority enrolments. On the other hand, teachers in schools with high minority enrolments were more likely than teachers in schools with minority enrolments of 6 to 20 percent to use these technologies at home to post homework or assignments.

Like minority enrolment, poverty concentration of the school is related to teachers' use of technology for communicative purposes. For example, teachers in schools with lower poverty concentrations were generally more likely than teachers in the highest poverty schools to use computers or the internet to communicate with colleagues.

Fifty-nine percent of teachers in schools with less than 11 percent, 55 percent of teacher in schools with 11 to 30 percent, and 54 percent of teachers in schools with 31 to 49 percent of students eligible for free or reduced-price school lunch used these technologies at school for this purpose, compared with 38 percent of teachers in schools with 71 percent or more students eligible for free or reduced-price school lunch. Similarly, 53 percent of teachers in schools with poverty concentrations of 11 to 30 percent eligible for free or reduced-price school lunch used these technologies at home to communicate with colleagues, compared with 40 percent of teachers in schools with 71 percent or more students eligible for free or reduced-price school lunch.

In addition to preparation for classroom instruction, administrative tasks, and communication, teachers may also use computers or the internet for a number of instructional activities in their classrooms.

The 1999 FRSS survey on public school teachers' use of technology asked teachers how often they used computers or the internet during class time and assigned students to use these technologies for projects and various other activities, including: word processing/ spreadsheets, internet research, practice drills, solving problems/analysing data, CD-ROM research, multimedia projects, graphical presentations, demonstration/ simulation, and correspondence with experts.

Fifty-three percent of public school teachers indicated that they used computers or the internet for instruction during class time. Elementary teachers were more likely to do this than secondary teachers, and teachers in schools with smaller enrolments were more likely to do this than teachers in schools with the largest enrolments.

Teachers in schools with lower minority enrolments were generally more likely to use computers or the internet for instruction during class time than teachers in schools with high minority enrolments. Similarly, teachers in the lowest poverty schools (based on percent of students eligible for free or reduced-price school lunch) were more likely than teachers in schools with 50 to 70 percent eligible students to use computers or the internet in this way.

Elementary teachers were more likely than secondary teachers to assign projects using the computer *inside* the classroom, and less likely than secondary teachers to assign projects using the computer *outside* of the classroom.

Teachers' use of technology for instructional activities varied by a number of school and teacher characteristics. For example, elementary teachers were more likely than secondary teachers to assign students to use computers or the internet to practice drills.

In addition, elementary teachers were more likely than secondary teachers to assign students to use these technologies to solve problems and analyse data. On the other hand, secondary teachers were more likely than elementary teachers to assign students to use these technologies to conduct research using the internet.

Teachers in schools with different enrolment sizes varied with respect to whether they assigned students to use computers or the internet for various instructional activities.

Teachers in schools with smaller enrolments were nearly twice as likely as teachers in schools with large enrolments to assign students to use these technologies to practice drills. Teachers in schools with smaller enrolments were also more likely than teachers in schools with the largest enrolments to assign students to use computers or the internet to solve problems and analyse data.

There were also differences in whether teachers assigned students to use technology for various instructional activities according to minority enrolment. For example, teachers in schools enroling the smallest proportion of minority students were more likely to assign students to use these technologies for word processing and creating spreadsheets than teachers in the highest minority enrolment schools.

Teachers in lower minority enrolment schools were also generally more likely than teachers in the highest minority enrolment schools to assign students to use these technologies for multimedia presentations and CD-ROM research. Finally, teachers in schools with smaller proportions of minority enrolments were more likely to use computers or the internet for internet research.

Similar to the differences in minority enrolment, school poverty concentration is related to a number of activities for which teachers assign students to use computers or the internet. Teachers in schools with the lowest poverty concentrations were more likely than teachers in schools with the highest poverty concentrations to assign students to use these technologies for graphical presentations, multimedia presentations, word processing and spreadsheets, research using CD-ROM and the internet, and corresponding with experts.

Design and Technology

Design and technology can be seen as having a considerable body of knowledge with which skills interact and from which product outcomes may duly arise. Within the National Curriculum for England and

Wales, this body of knowledge and understanding of materials and components can be classified broadly within areas such as the working characteristics of materials and combinations of materials; use of mechanism including control, and switching with electric circuits.

These areas embrace an ocean of conceptual matters and real-life experience and are founded on the interrelationships between the great scientific abstractions of matter, energy and force.

Structures are necessarily encountered in many aspects of children's activity in designing and making. Activities involving the arrangement of materials so they retain their shape when subjected to forces will have a structural dimension. This applies as much to modelling a house in card or paper as it does to the baking of bread or the building of a car or tower with a construction kit: all these products retain their shape despite the influence of say, gravitational or frictional forces. The publication of a subject-specific Design and Technology guidance scheme of work by the UK government agency, the Qualifications and Curriculum Authority of the Department for Education and Employment. (QCA/ DfEE) underpins the relevance of this broad influence of structures on designing and making activity.

Within this scheme, nine out of the range of 24 classroom planning units feature some aspect of structures as the main or shared focal point. It is worth noting however, that the QCA/ DfEE scheme of work was founded upon a pre-1999 version of the national curriculum for England and Wales and does not reflect the revised, relatively low density level of knowledge and understanding now required of children aged 3-11 engaged in design and technology in English and Welsh schools.

For comparison from an American perspective, a set of Standards now define and detail content for the study of technology to significant depth. Areas specific to the understanding of structures (for children in Grades 3-5) can be found under Core Concepts, Standard 2, where it is noted that "The properties of a specific material determine whether it is suitable for a given application", and in Standard 20, Construction Technologies, where "The type of structure determines how the parts are put together".

The QCA/DfEE guidance materials have been widely adopted by schools for children in the age range 3-11 in England and Wales. It is this widespread adoption of a government-approved scheme of work that would appear to bring with it a considerable classroom commitment to the teaching of structures.

Concern for teacher understanding in the area of structures has become evident with the publication of formal teacher education and self-study materials by higher education and UK government agencies. These materials have been intended for use by teachers in schools, often using classroom ideas from children as links to the misunderstanding of concepts relating to forces held by adults, and thus of course, teachers. A self-study guide on Forces has within it a dedicated section on structures to assist teacher understanding. This resource is prefaced by a carefully worded caveat to the effect that the purpose of the material is to extend teacher knowledge and understanding and that it is not suitable for direct use in the classroom. Clearly, some degree of background knowledge beyond the working level of children is seen as desirable.

Teacher understanding specific to design and technology has been highlighted by the UK Teacher Training Agency with the publication of self-assessment texts intended to provide diagnostic feedback for serving teachers.

Recent changes in the requirements for the qualification of teachers in England and Wales have further underpinned this subject-specific deepening of teacher knowledge. All student teachers in England and Wales now have to comply with certain specified Standards regarding background knowledge in subject areas if they are to gain qualified teacher status. It is interesting to note that nationally defined curriculum specifications for children's learning have been reduced and yet the reverse is true for teachers.

The government-specified standards in science require that trainees for school teaching of ages 3-11 should "...identify how the different areas of science relate to each other (unifying principles and concepts), so that they can make conceptual links across the subject, present pupils with a coherent perspective of the subject matter taught, and ensure progression in pupil's learning". This is a significant demand on student teachers. Clearly it is insufficient for them to simply possess knowledge of say, forces or energy. Instead they should develop an understanding of the interaction of these underlying principles. This is a conceptually challenging requirement.

Work embracing ideas on structures can be seen as having dual purposes in the assembling of knowledge and understanding. It may serve to combine knowledge and experience of the properties of materials with an understanding of forces acting on the materials.

At a classroom level, when children are engaged in design-and-make activities, such as modelling buildings in card or paper, they are using a sheet material that can be shaped so that it is able to offer resistance to certain forces. As a consequence, the card can maintain its shape for presentational and structural purposes. The act of putting a crease or bend in a piece of sheet material is significant and the rationale behind this action may be based on the notion that "bends make certain things stronger."

In the light of ideas such as this, questioning and observation of actions of student teachers in design and technology workshops has provided some useful evidence. It has shown ways in which thinking and past experience have played a part in shaping responses and serves to indicate levels of conceptual grasp. In particular, some previously formed ideas that student teachers carry to new learning situations can exert significant influence.

A considerable research arena has been built up around the issue of what, in literature stemming from science education, cognitive science, and developmental psychology, may be termed "misconceptions". These have been succinctly described as situations arising from the ways that "children and adults construct their own ideas about natural phenomena that are often different from scientists' ideas".

The term "misconception" is but one of many descriptors for this phenomenon. Other terms include "preconceptions" and "children's ideas". Generally these descriptors can be seen within the scope of a theory of knowledge and learning recognised by the genetic epistemologist as one of continuous construction since "in each act of understanding, some degree of invention is involved; in development, the passage from one stage to the next is always characterised by the formation of new structures which did not exist before, either in the external world or in the subject's mind".

The philosophical underpinning of the theory of continuous construction, or constructivism, contrasts sharply with other perspectives. Among these can be identified the notion of empiricism, in which discoveries, although new to the subjects making them, are already perceived to have existed in reality and did not result in the construction of new realities. Another view is that of the nativist or a priorist. This asserts the predetermination of forms of knowledge inside the subject.

Misconceptions can be seen to arise as part of the process of continuous construction. They represent mental models, constructed by individuals who have used whatever evidence has been at hand, that are at odds with the views held by the majority of members of a community of knowledge.

A significant body of research has been conducted on the basis of investigating children's misconceptions. However it is reasonable to assume that misconceptions reside in adults, too, and that inappropriate ideas left unchallenged in children will persist into adulthood.

A perception within the constructivist view of education is that appropriate elicitation of ideas may expose misconceptions. Subsequent learning experiences may provide settings to challenge misconceived ideas and so promote conceptual shift towards that held by a majority of participants in a community of knowledge, such as scientists. It could be said, for example, that the more "scientific" an individual becomes may be due to the enhanced opportunities they have had to gain and analyse evidence and set this against the ideas they already hold. This cannot happen in isolation. Opportunities to discuss ideas and effectively form localized communities of knowledge through small-group discussions would appear to be part of a "sense-making" pathway to enhanced understanding.

The notion of constructivism can be taken further into a broad philosophical arena with the assertion that, "Radical constructivism, thus, is radical because it breaks with convention and develops a theory of knowledge in which knowledge does not reflect an "objective" ontological reality, but exclusively an ordering and organisation of a world constituted by our experience".

Such construction of the individual's subjective reality possesses not only elements assembled through personal actions, but also the influence of prevailing social and environmental conditions. A logical, and perhaps disturbing endpoint of this line of thought can be determined. If social and radical constructivism deny the existence of an objectivist, ontological reality, then this metaphysical and epistemological denial "effectively opposes the basis of knowledge for science and social studies education as well as the knowledge which helps to structure the organisation of schooling itself".

The notion of strength and how and where forces may act are central to student understanding of structures. Student teachers will carry their own ideas about these concepts and some of them will be misconceived. One of the principal misconceptions revolves around the notion of "reaction forces." Learners do not readily appear to recognise that forces act in pairs and that as a consequence of a force acting upon a structure, the structure will react in opposition to the applied force. This can be seen as a fundamental plank in terms of the pathway to understanding since "Only when more than one force is recognised can thinking about equilibrium start".

Minstrell in his study of high school physics students demonstrated that only half of a classroom sample suggested that a table might "push back" on an overlying book. From the Minstrell evidence it seems that even young adults in the specialised learning environment of a physics class will cling to previous ideas. Within the development of student teacher's expanding body of knowledge it is possible, then, for a range of misconceptions to persist into and beyond their training environments and thus indeed into the classroom. Research evidence collected from children in. the 7-11 age range for the SPACE research reports similarly substantiates the widely held misconception relating to reaction forces.

The role of problem-solving has early links with the evolution of "technology" älater resolved from information technology to become Design and Technology in the English and Welsh curriculum. Various key texts have had a profound influence on shaping the minds of young designers, their teachers, and curriculum developers alike. Notable among these is Johnsey's model of problem-solving in school science with its fundamental contextual links between technology and science.

Problem-solving as a means of learning has a host of benefits including task ownership, cross-curricular activity, and communication enhancement. A group-based social setting for problem-solving was employed which had numerous benefits in terms of role-finding and the sharing of ideas.

Furthermore, within these social settings, language flowed freely and informal tutor eavesdropping, as well as more direct questioning of groups, revealed much about the how the quality of thought, prior experience, and on-task conceptual reshaping had impacted the problem-solving situation.

The problem was focused on an apparently simple bridge-building task, using limited materials. The use of limited materials had a direct effect in terms of guiding participants towards a variety of structural solutions. The problem was based upon an idea from a seminal work produced by the Berkshire Local Education Authority featuring child-centered designing-and-making, problem-solving situations sketched out for direct use in classrooms.

The focal point activity offered to students in this study was actually an extension of one of the examples taken from this text. The problem, centered upon a popular children's folk tale entitled "The Three Billy Goats Gruff," is framed with these words:

"The Troll was so angry at the three Billy Goats Gruff crossing the bridge and eating his green grass that he demolished the bridge. To stop the goats making a new bridge he removed all the wood from the river bank and has left some paper behind because he does not think the goats could make a paper bridge".

Conditions are then attached to this task for children. They are to model the bridge across a gap of 25 cm. They can use only 3 sheets of letter size paper (210 X

296 mm) and goats made of modelling clay of specified masses must be able to make the crossing. For the purposes of this study the Billy Goat problem was utilised for work with student teachers. Changes in the structural specification were made in order to provide challenge at an adult level. Student teachers were thus required to work to an enhanced set of performance criteria attached to the following task: "Design and make a structure across a 40 cm gap so that it may be traversed by a (specified) simple vehicle.

The structure must be capable of supporting a 50 g mass at its center, but not when the vehicle is crossing." Additional design criteria were specified to enhance the problem-solving setting such as: "The structure will enable you to give the simple vehicle one push on one side of the gap. It should then traverse the gap on its wheels so that it arrives on the other side still travelling on wheels" and " You may only use paper clips and A4 sheets of paper to build the structure."

Further conditions on construction techniques were specified such as "You may not use any other materials. You may not pierce the sides of the intervening gap to fix paper clips. You can cut the paper with scissors." Finally economic specifications were added such as "Paper clips cost £3 each. Paper costs £10 per sheet" and " The budget limit for the task is £100. You may experiment with unlimited supplies of paper and paper clips ät he budget applies to the finished structure".

Further challenge to the problem-solving task was provided with an economic dimension. Although a budget had been set, clearly if bridges could be constructed which met the criteria and undercut the £100 limit then these could be seen as being economically advantageous. As an ongoing task, students who met the initial criteria refined their designs and considered other possibilities with lower cost implications.

On the whole it would seem desirable that misconceptions are challenged and reconstructed in student teacher training sessions. The more active student teachers become in the construction of their own knowledge, the more able they may be to appreciate the breadth and significance of constructivist learning theory and how it may be applied to enhance the learning of the children they will teach. Additionally, the more that the knowledge of the student teacher is constructed along the lines of the scientific community, the less likely it is that these future teachers will foster the development of inappropriate conceptual frameworks in the minds of the children they will teach.

Experimental Learning

Experiential, or experience-based learning can be regarded as the earliest approach to learning for the human race, the significance and potential of it has not been fully recognised until relatively recently. In the formal education system it has tended to be developed and regarded as somehow fundamentally inferior to those organised forms of knowledge which have been constructed as subjects or disciplines. The practical and the applied do not tend to have the same status in educational institutions as the academic and the abstract.

Interestingly, scholars from outside of youth education often have a more sanguine contribution to make in defining how people learn. Adult education scholars, for example, have found it constructive to document the learning process for adults as experiential. What these authors do is provide alternative ways of looking at the question of how people learn, resulting in a productive view of the learning process among humans, both young and old, about which there is a reasonable degree of consensus.

Kolb argued that defining learning in terms of the change in behaviour is limiting and it poorly characterises the learning process. Kolb defined learning as a human adaptation process. "It is a process whereby knowledge is created through the transformation of experience". He cited Lewin's work as the empirical evidence for supporting a learning cycle theory that begins with the experiences of the learner. Lewin's formula for learning describes human behaviour as a function of a person and the environment. Learning takes place, according to Lewin, when a learner (person) interacts with, or is stimulated by, an environment. Others adopt the same human adaptation process' explanation for learning, but cast it in different ways. Jarvis, for example, put it this way: "...there is no meaning in a given situation until we relate our own experiences to it".

Experience plays a key role in the process. Rogers has been quite outspoken about the learning process, especially the role of a teacher in that process. He believes no one learns anything of significance from someone else. Instead, learning takes place when a learner is intrinsically motivated to learn and undertakes to learn something on his/her own. This sentiment is echoed by Albert Einstein who was quoted as saying: "I never teach my pupils; I only attempt to provide the conditions in which they can learn". In short, there appears to be more clarity and conviction about what constitutes learning among people outside of the formal education field than in it.

To reach their conclusions about how people learn, these scholars make reference to quantitative and qualitative studies with human subjects. They follow the canons of science to clarify and verify what they believe to be true. A contrasting method for exploring the learning phenomenon is to trust in one's own experience. Beginning with Boud's broader perspective of how people learn, the following analysis attempts to do this from first principles. It represents an attempt to trust experience in apposition to, or in contrast with, the rules of scientific inquiry. The remainder of the paper draws on two more pragmatic forms of inquiry for its analysis. Following a review of some recent literature on what constitutes learning, conceptual analysis and comparative analysis will be used to explicate the essence of experiential learning.

Traditional pedagogy tends to assume the acquisition of knowledge and understanding by the mind is a passive exercise. Psychological research and theory perpetuates this tradition by dividing the person into body and mind, into active and passive processes. Insufficient attention is paid to combinations of these categories. The result is a gap between what experience tells us about how we learn and what the experts tell us. "Thought and action tend to have been separated, thinking and understanding to have been seen as abstract and general, therefore as teachable in abstract isolation from practical experience.

In contrast, practical competence has often been spoken of as though it were just a matter of doing; skill is then taken to mean a combination of thoughtless behaviour habits, inculcatable through simple practice". The momentum associated with this view is so deeply imbedded in teacher education methods and curriculum that it has seldom been challenged, until recently that is.

Harre and Gillett in a book entitled *The Discursive Mind* challenged the prevailing view of how people retain what they learn. In a chapter entitled, "The Discursive Origins of the Sense of Self," the authors suggested that learning a language, i.e., learning signs and symbols, does not give human beings a sense of physical location. "It is the learning of perceptual and motor skills that is responsible for that". Human beings, they suggest, live in two worlds:

One world is essentially discursive in character, that is, it is a world of signs and symbol subject to normative constraints. [The second is the material or physical world]. There are two main kinds of skills that are often brought into play together and in complementary ways [within these two worlds]. There are manual skills, those we use to manipulate material stuff, and there are discursive skills, those we use in our symbolic interactions. The world of symbols is organised by the norms and conventions of correct symbol use. The other world in which we live, the physical or material world, is structured by causal processes. Our language is our main means for managing in the world of symbols, our hands and brains are in the material world. This analysis may help explain the experiential frame of reference preferred by technological education teachers. These teachers have lived and worked extensively in the material world developing their problem solving and manual skills. They often become socialised into a way of learning that is different from that used in the schools.

In some respects learning and practising technology are synonymous activities to them. Human development in its fullest sense requires that people learn to function effectively in the discursive world but as a complement to the material world, rather than in opposition to it or apart from it. These technology teachers may, in fact, be applying a learning methodology which has implications for understanding how people learn but which is overlooked in the educational sciences.

The ramifications of this observation are amusing and perplexing at the same time. What would a curriculum which blends the discursive and non-discursive worlds look like? The sense of self that Harre and Gillett described brings the role of the teacher and the role of experience in learning into clearer focus. Their position that the sense of self and learning/development are unified through experience is intriguing:

The discursive thesis is that to experience oneself as having a location in a manifold of places and in relation to others is a necessary condition for being able to use and to understand indexical expressions. How does it come about that these senses of unique location are the salient features of selfhood? We do not believe that learning a language is what is responsible for our having the sense of physical location. It is the learning of perceptual and motor skills that is responsible for that.

We think that the sense of a genetic position, the sense that one is the agent of one's actions and responsible to others for them, is something that we acquire through learning the language and cultural conventions for the assignment of responsibility. These aspects of the sense of the self physical location, temporal continuity, and agency-have different origins but they come together in the grammar. According to Vygotsky, the learning of manual skills is just as much a necessary condition for acquiring a sense of self as the learning of verbal skills. We believe that perception is a kind of manual skill. The ability to use your eyes is a bit like the ability to use your hands. In living our lives as members of a community that inhabits physical space and time, and assesses each of its members for reliability, these centerings come together.

Several years earlier Carl Rogers speculated that sense of self was important when he stated that a person learns significantly only those things which he or she perceives as being involved in the maintenance of, or enhancement of, the structure of self. It would seem that skill development is crucial to one's learning and that it should be integrated with, not separated from, learning of signs and symbols, e.g., the alphabet, numbers, words, etc., a fact that technological education teachers have known for years. But why is this knowledge not more widely researched/analysed, and recognised?

Analysing Experiential Learning

Conceptual analysis as a technique is used by philosophers to analyse illusive phenomena. By asking "what" questions and relentlessly dissecting the answers until a residue can be identified, they attempt to reveal the truth about a phenomenon. The methodology employs a test known as the necessary and sufficient conditions test. In this instance, what would be the necessary and sufficient conditions for experiential learning to exist? Experiential learning was defined as learning which combined mental, emotional, and physiological stimuli. These necessary and sufficient conditions for experiential learning were organised and distilled from a range of individual and group responses. There must be a balance of aural, visual, tactile, olfactory, and emotional stimuli.

Learning involves observing, doing, or living through things (it is associated with skill development, practical knowledge, and action: the result or residue of experiential learning is the long term memory associated with it).

Intrinsic motivation transcends extrinsic motivation.

— The learner, in some significant respect, is the initiator of the learning.
— The learning process, in some respect, is perceived to be controlled by the learner.
— The goals of the learning process, to some extent, are thought to be the learner's goals.
— Accountability for the learning act or actions is the perceived province of the learner.

Analysis and reflection are a significant part of the learning act, i.e., the learner values what he/she is learning and there is an extension to that learning (the analysis and reflection gained from an experience extend it to a larger context and vice-versa).

The nature of the learning process itself is such that it is often associated with objectivity, subjectivity, and open-endedness. There is sustainability and consistency associated with the learning (the learning act is not characterised as being associated with immediacy—there is no deliberate recall or time-line associated with learning).

The conditions under which experiential learning were thought to exist by these teacher candidates are often contradictory to what is considered common knowledge about how children learn in school or how they should be taught. The belief that learning is a trial and error process provides one example. Children quickly learn in school that there are right and wrong answers to most questions.

Most knowledge is abstracted in such a way that it can be digested in small doses, avoiding knowledge about phenomena that are difficult to define or quantify.

Yet beyond a fundamental base of knowledge or literacy/numeracy, living is very much a subjective trial and error process which requires a balance of factual and practical knowledge, much of which is about 'best' solutions, not right versus wrong answers. Most technologists and many technological education teachers know this general truth and apply it in their own learning/teaching.

Another way of defining something from first principles is to compare and contrast it with a phenomenon that it is not. This technique is referred to by scholars as comparative analysis. Comparative researchers will often begin their studies by setting up a juxtaposition then search for a unifying concept and hypothesis to illuminate it.

For example, if learning is such an elusive concept to define, why not try to analyse what it means by comparing it to other known concepts. In this instance a comparison of what it means "to study" versus "to experience" might reveal what learning is thought to be. Could such an analysis reveal the real essence of learning? What does it mean to experience something as opposed to study it? What is the relationship of these two distinct actions and how do they impact on learning?

To study, according the Canadian Senior Dictionary is to learn or gain knowledge by means of books, observation, or experiment. To experience is to live through something, to act, to do, to respect, to suffer the consequences of, to feel, to internalise something. Could the act of studying be an aspect of experiencing? Experiencing may involve studying but it is unlikely that studying, by itself, would meet all the criteria for being called experiential learning.

Yet studying has a speculative aspect to it that transcends experience in some way. The process speaks to a way of learning or thinking that is unique. It need not be utilitarian to be useful. The purposes for which study is intended determine its utility. Often this is a very personal process.

The object of one's study may have no universal appeal at all, but it is still useful to the individual who initiated it. Study, then, is often contemplative in nature. Experience, by comparison, is practical in nature.

Scholars from Finland recently completed a comparative analysis which helps show how study and learning are related. In their analysis they attempt to describe how teachers perceive the learning process. What happens in schools, in their opinion, can best be described as "study." Kansanen et al., define study as what students do in response to teacher initiatives.

While they do not define the role of experience directly and how it relates to learning through study, they do refer to two different and important conceptions of knowledge, i.e., episteme versus phronesis, which are central to understanding that role. The dominating conception of rationality in educational sciences has been knowledge as episteme instead of knowledge as phronesis.

Kessels and Korthagen described knowledge from an epistemological view to be general by nature and usually formulated in abstract terms. Such knowledge is essentially conceptual. From the phronesis perspective a different picture emerges. Knowledge is mainly concerned with the understanding of concrete cases and complex situations. It [phronesis] considers knowledge as variable and essentially perceptual rather than conceptual.

Kansanen et al., point out that teachers' views of knowledge are central to what happens in their classrooms in terms of a practical versus academic orientation. Kansanen et al., have analysed carefully what they consider teachers' pedagogical thinking to be. One way to consider teachers' thinking, they suggest, is from the different perspectives on knowledge that they [teachers] adopt in their practice.

Whether or not beginning teachers reach a level of understanding which enables them to articulate and apply concepts like episteme and phronesis to the art of teaching is, according to Kansanen et al, open to question.

However, evidence suggests that teachers do have preconceptions which serve to define how they teach and what they believe about how young people learn.

The sources of those beliefs provides part of the explanation for the dissonance some technological education teachers' feel. It may be that technological education teachers think learning to be more practical while their counterparts in other school subjects consider learning to be more contemplative, two distinct but explainable views which have implications for understanding how people learn best.

The Kessels and Korthagen reference and Kansanen et al. analysis are integral to understanding the role of experience in learning. Teachers' views of knowledge and the episteme versus phronesis analysis helps illuminate how experience stimulates, animates, authenticates, and reinforces learning.

The practical capacity of human thought that the phronesis notion captures (where episteme does not) in conjunction with the sense of physical location argument provides the framework for understanding the role of experience in learning. It may also provide a rationale for practical subjects in schools, or even more important, a rationale for the use of experiential learning orientations by teachers in a wide range of subjects.

The experiences of technological education teachers may be particularly important to study if the curriculum in schools is to reflect the multidimensional needs of both young and mature learners and if a more complete understanding of how people learn is to be reached.

Many technological education teachers have a life and work experience base from which to draw when designing learning activities in schools. More important, this base is much more central to the effectiveness of these teachers and to curriculum design generally than heretofore thought. Such teachers and the teacher educators who prepare them initially for the role of teacher would do well to ensure this aspect of professional life is valued and recognised more widely.

Walter and Marks suggested that, qualitatively speaking, half of an individual's reality resides in action. The difficult time some students have with their learning in general often has to do with how they perceive themselves in relation to that learning. Our centerings as human beings are varied and complex as Harre and Gillett's work suggests. A combination of discursive and non-discursive orientations which serves all learners may be the solution.

From a systems perspective, making experience a central element in school curriculum would mean that writing curriculum would change dramatically. Learning outcomes would likely be more difficult to articulate. Their achievement by students would be less controlled and less controllable.

In the context of increasing teacher accountability, reducing teacher control on a system-wide basis could be a recipe for disorder if not chaos. On the other hand, interests outside of and inside the schooling infrastructure are calling for greater relevance in the curriculum and an experiential curriculum could be the answer.

Chapter 5

Technology Education Worldwide

The involvement of global media networks in providing higher education has been overstated, the research found ample evidence of individual projects and gathering focus on the use of new media and technology in higher education by established and new higher education institutions, and clear indications that this use will continue to grow. In some instances, major computer hardware and software companies are acting as a catalyst for change, providing expertise and resources to institutions to encourage them to adopt technology in their administrative and academic endeavours. In this respect, the companies are seeking to establish a presence as a carrier, rather than a provider, of educational content.

The use of technology and new media is in many cases still in its experimental stages. While it is facilitating expansion into distance education by many higher education providers (including traditional universities) and brokers, such as the Western Governors University in the United States, and the rhetoric is global, the focus is in most cases at this stage on a local or at best national market. This may well change in the future, as programs become established and appropriate technological infrastructure becomes more widely available. There are already several examples of small-scale master of business administration (MBA) courses which enrol students internationally and which employ a variety of media and technologies.It must also be said that there are new providers emerging, and that some of these have global aspirations. Many originate in North America, in contexts that differ significantly from the Australian environment. For example, the use of the word 'university' is regulated in Australia. In the United States, many organisations use the word in circumstances that differ from the Australian understanding of the term.

There is evidence of a major segmentation of the market, with new providers targeting the 'lifelong learning' cohort. This includes corporate training/ education, a domain only partially catered for by traditional universities, and a profitable market—being largely self-funded and employer-funded. Continuing and professional education is a component of lifelong learning for those in the workforce. There is a widespread perception that traditional institutions are not meeting the needs of the lifelong learning cohort and that the field is open for new providers to meet market demands.

One obvious, and problematic, outcome of this segmentation is that traditional institutions may be left serving the less-profitable traditional undergraduate market, which is largely government-funded or family-funded, in a time when governments are increasingly endeavouring to cut public outlays. Looking further into the future than the medium-term prospects, this arguably represents one of the most significant challenges to, and opportunities for, established higher education providers.

Converging technologies and the potential for global reach have led some to assume the existence of one 'global market'. Conversely, this investigation would support the notion of the fragmentation of world markets and the development of numerous niche markets on an international and regional, rather than global scale. There is no 'blanket' approach to delivery of a global education program and that the education providers who identify their niche and meet the demands of the relevant stakeholders are those that will be best placed in a global marketplace.

The development of high-performance computing and communications is creating new media, such as the World Wide Web and virtual reality. In turn, these new media enable new types of messages and experiences; for example, interpersonal interactions in immersive, synthetic environments lead to the formation of virtual communities. The innovative kinds of pedagogy empowered by these emerging media, messages, and experiences make possible a transformation of conventional distance education—which replicates traditional classroom teaching across barriers of distance and time—into an alternative instructional paradigm: distributed learning.

What does the evolution of new media mean for distance educators? A medium is in part a channel for conveying content; new media such as the internet allow us to readily reach wider, more diverse audiences. Just as important, however, is that a medium is a representational container enabling new types of messages (e.g., a picture is worth a thousand words). Because the process of thinking is based on representations like language and imagery, the process of learning is strongly shaped by the types of instructional messages we can exchange with students. Emerging representational containers like hypermedia enable a broader, more powerful repertoire of pedagogical strategies.

The global marketplace and the communications and entertainment industries are driving the rapid evolution of high-performance computing and communications. Regional, national, and global information infrastructures are being developed to enhance our abilities to sense, act, and learn across barriers of distance and time. The ways in which information is created, delivered, and used in business, government, and society are swiftly changing. To successfully prepare students as workers and citizens, educators must incorporate experiences creating and utilising new forms of expression, such as multimedia, in the curriculum. Information infrastructures offer channels for delivering these technology-intensive learning experiences to any place on demand.

The information superhighway metaphor now widely used to convey the implications of high-performance computing and communications is inadequate. Such an analogy is the equivalent of someone in 1896 declaring that the airplane will be the canal system of the 20th century.

Backward-looking metaphors focus on what we can automate—how we can use channels to send conventional forms of content more efficiently—but they miss the true innovation: redefining how we communicate and educate by using new types of messages and experiences to be more effective. Because emerging forms of representation such as hypermedia and virtual reality are in the early stages of development, we are just beginning to understand how they shape not only their messages but their users.

Many people are still reeling from the first impact of high-performance computing and communications—shifting from the challenge of not getting enough information to the challenge of surviving too much information. The core skill for today's workplace is not foraging for data but filtering a plethora of incoming information.

The emerging literacy we all must master requires diving into a sea of information and immersing ourselves in data in order to harvest patterns of knowledge, just as fish extract oxygen from water with their gills. As educators, understanding how to structure learning experiences to make such immersion possible is the core of the new rhetoric. Expanding traditional definitions of literacy and rhetoric into immersion-centered experiences of interacting with information is crucial to preparing students for full participation in 21st-century society.

Conventional distance education is similar to traditional classroom instruction except that it uses technology-based delivery systems. In contrast, emerging forms of distributed learning are leading to a reconceptualisation of education's mission, clients, process, and content. This new instructional paradigm is based on shifts in what learners need to be prepared for the future as well as on new capabilities in the pedagogical repertoire of teachers. The following four new forms of expression are shaping the emergence of distributed learning as a new pedagogical model.

i) Knowledge webs complement teachers, texts, libraries, and archives as sources of information.

ii) Interactions in virtual communities complement face-to-face relationships in classrooms.

iii) Experiences in synthetic environments extend learning-by-doing in real-world settings.

iv) Sensory immersion helps learners grasp reality through illusion.

Using information infrastructures, educators and students can join distributed conferences that provide an instant network of contacts who have useful skills and immediate answers to questions. In time, these informal sources of expertise will utilise embedded groupware tools to enhance collaboration. On the internet, online archival resources are increasingly linked to the World Wide Web, accessible through webcrawlers like Mosaic and Netscape.

Eventually, artificial-intelligence-based guides will facilitate navigating through huge amounts of stored information. Virtual exhibits that duplicate real-world settings (e.g., museums) are emerging; these environments make a wide variety of experiences possible without the necessity of travel or scheduling. Distributed science projects enable shared experiments to be conducted across time and space, with each team member learning more about the phenomenon being studied and about scientific investigation than would be possible in isolation. Combined, all these capabilities to enhance information-gathering and creation form knowledge webs. However, access to data does not automatically expand students' knowledge; the availability of information does not intrinsically create an internal framework of ideas that learners can use to interpret reality.

Although presentational approaches transmit material rapidly from source to student, this content often evaporates quickly from learners' minds. To be motivated to master concepts and skills, students need to see the connection between what they are learning and the rest of their lives and the mental models they already use. Even when learners are drilled in a topic until facts are indefinitely retained—we all know that the sum of a triangle's internal angles is 180 degrees—this knowledge is often "inert;" most people don't know how to apply the abstract principles they memorised in school to real-world problems. To move students from assimilating inert facts into generating mental models, teachers must structure learning experiences that highlight how new ideas can provide insights in intriguing and challenging situations.

The curriculum is already overcrowded with low-level information; teachers frantically race through required material, helping students memorise factual data to be regurgitated on mandated, standardised tests. Using information infrastructures as a fire hose to spray more information into educational settings would make this situation even worse. Without skilled facilitation, many learners who access current knowledge webs will flounder in a morass of unstructured data.

A vital, emerging form of literacy that educators must communicate is how to transform archival information into personal knowledge. However, moving students from access through assimilation to appropriation requires educational experiences that empower knowledge construction by unsophisticated learners, helping them make sense of massive, incomplete, and inconsistent information sources. Weaving learner-centered, constructivist usage of linked, online materials into the curriculum and culture of traditional educational institutions is the next stage of evolution for conventional distance education.

Modular Technology Education

Modular technology education (MTE) defined as a "self-contained instructional system for self-directed, individualised instruction." MTE is generally thought of as a curriculum provided by a commercial vendor in which students learn about an area of technology by:

(a) participating in interactive media presentations,

(b) following instructions in workbooks,

(c) writing responses in student journals, and

(d) experimenting and building projects.

Working in pairs, students complete instructional activities at computerised work stations. Students follow self-directed instructions that introduce and reinforce technological concepts. Many MTE curricula have a strong "hands-on" component in which students use tools to process resources, generally resulting in a completed prototype or experiment.

Personal computers are replacing the classroom teacher as the disseminator of technological content and processes in modular programs. The modular approach is relatively new to our profession and largely untested as to its instructional efficacy. Furthermore, MTE is replacing traditional technology education programs at an unprecedented rate. In an effort to determine the prevalence of MTE programs in America's public schools, the following strategies were pursued:

a) the main MTE companies, in terms of market share, were contacted relative to numbers of installed labs,

b) data were compiled relative to secondary school counts, and

c) percentage frequencies were calculated for middle and high school MTE facilities.

Representatives from eight companies were contacted. An MTE lab consists of eight or more modular work stations with a computerised management system. Six of the eight companies contacted were willing to reveal the number of MTE labs that they have installed as of September 2001. Among the six responding companies, there were 5,088 middle-level and 2,177 high school MTE labs.

The researcher has determined the existence of 17,542 public middle/ intermediate schools in America and 15,391 high schools. Middle/intermediate school numbers were compiled by adding secondary school counts by states in Patterson's American Education 2000 edition data for grades 5-9, 7-12, and K-12. Data for high schools were compiled by adding data for grades 7-12, 9-12, 10-12, and K-12. Dividing 5,088 by 17,542 indicates that 29% of American middle/intermediate school contain a modular program. Similarly, dividing 2,177 by 15,391 indicates that 14% of American high schools have modular programs. These MTE frequency data are conservative estimates since only about three-quarters of the major MTE companies provided data and because both 7-12 and K-12 schools were used in calculating both middle/intermediate frequency and high school frequency numbers. These data support the widespread adoption of MTE across the US.

Through observation and teaching experience in a modular lab, the researcher has observed variance in students' ability to master the learning tasks presented via the computer-assisted instruction (CAI) used in MTE. Some students excel in modular programs while others struggle. What characteristics do students possess that enable them to become proficient at mastering the learning experiences presented in MTE? Conversely, how can technology education teachers, administrators, and MTE program developers address the needs of students at risk of failing to grasp the content presented in this learning environment?

As the modular approach replaces traditional technology education programs, questions arise concerning how students' individual traits and characteristics interact with the learning tasks presented in this instructional paradigm. Limited research has been conducted regarding these relationships.

Traditionally, schools emphasise the use of externally supplied rewards and punishments as a means of controlling behavior and in directing the learning process. Modular programs, however, require a shift away from external motivation strategies in which students are rewarded and punished by the teacher. MTE programs, with their self-paced CAI instructional approach, require students to be intrinsically motivated. MTE posttest scores from a unit on engineering structures taught by CAI. Continuous (i.e., interval level) data were collected with a fifty point MTE posttest instrument developed by the researcher.

The independent variables were:

(a) academic ability with two levels of continuous data, including verbal and quantitative ability;

(b) achievement motivation with one level of continuous data;

(c) cognitive style with three levels of categorical data, including field dependent, field intermediate, and field independent, and one level of continuous data (i.e., raw scores), and

(d) prior knowledge with one level of continuous data reported as students' pretest scores.

Subjects participated in three multimedia CAI activities over four class periods. The researcher monitored subjects' progress to ensure equivalent exposure to all material presented in the CAI lessons. The domain of knowledge included information about:

(a) types of bridges and structures,

(b) forces and loads,

(c) impacts of structures,

(d) construction cost and time,

(e) various road conditions,

(f) careers, and

(g) a unit review.

A 50 point posttest, identical to the pretest, was administered after the final multimedia presentation. The posttest was administered within four days of the final computer mediated presentation. Cognitive style of the subjects was determined through the Group Embedded Figures Test (GEFT). The motivation of the subjects was determined through the Children's Academic Intrinsic Motivation Instrument (CAIMI). The CAI multimedia presentations consisted of narrated text, music, sound effects, video animations, photographs, and hypertext links. Activities started with directions presented on the computer monitor. Consistent with the instructional design of the module, dyads navigated the multimedia presentations at their own rate.

The computer program used to presented several multimedia selections. Subjects were stopped by the CAI program to answer questions in an electronic journal. The CAI program summarised the material presented in each lesson. The researcher observed that many subjects were not following the CAI program in the proper instructional order and appeared to be confused. The researcher used a checklist to monitor progress and insure equal access to the CAI instruction.

Statistically significant relationships were demonstrated in the bivariate analysis between the MTE posttest and:

(a) cognitive style as measured with the GEFT instrument;

(b) quantitative ability and verbal ability as measured with subjects' fifth-grade CTP III test scores;

(c) prior knowledge as measured with the pretest; and

(d) motivation as measured with the CAIMI intrinsic motivation instrument.

The bivariate analysis also revealed statistically significant differences between the FIM and FI and the FD and FI cognitive style groups relative to MTE posttest performance. The magnitude of the relationships between students' posttest scores with verbal ability and prior knowledge was surprising. As bivariate predictors, verbal ability accounted for 53.5% and prior knowledge 55.1% of the total MTE posttest variance in this sample.

Multiple regression was used in the multivariate analysis to determine the existence of relationships between MTE posttest scores (dependent variable) and the students' cognitive style, verbal ability, quantitative ability, and intrinsic motivation (independent variables). Based upon the bivariate analysis, it is reasonable to conclude that verbal ability and prior knowledge enable a student to do better on the MTE posttest.

Quantitative ability, cognitive style, and intrinsic motivation correlated significantly with MTE posttest scores in the bivariate analysis. However, these variables "washed out" in the multivariate analysis. The predictor variables used in the multivariate analysis did not show multicollinearity with each other.

CAIMI displayed a low correlation with MTE posttest scores in the bivariate analysis. The CAIMI variable may not have been an accurate measurement of the intrinsic motivation construct. The multiple regression model developed to determine whether students were at risk in terms of MTE achievement.

A profile for low achieving students was developed in this analysis; the identification and remediation of "MTE low-achievers" was one objective of this research project. This profile was defined as students having scores one standard deviation below the mean on the MTE pretest, CTP III verbal and quantitative ability tests, GEFT cognitive style instrument, and CAIMI intrinsic motivation instrument.

Technology Education in Finnish Primary Schools

Finland has a long tradition of teaching practical school subjects. Since 1866, educational handwork (sloyd) has been a compulsory school subject for both boys and girls. Finnish technology education, called "technical work" in the national curriculum guidelines, is a school subject in which pupils design and make products by using different materials, machines, processes, techniques and tools. This emphasis on designing and making is an essential part of Finnish technology education. It is believed that such experiences develop pupils' knowledge, personal qualities, and psychomotor skills. As with the traditional (sloyd) programs that preceded it, there is general belief that the design and build approach used in contemporary technology education programs enhances the pupils' creativity, dexterity, diligence, initiative, problem solving, self-image, and preparation for work.

As technology education has evolved in Finland, more content has been introduced, including such areas as electricity, electronics, machinery, and computers. Construction kits for teaching control technology have also been adopted. In addition, technology education classes now offers pupils the opportunity to service and repair their bicycles, mopeds, and other technical equipment. These areas, combined with the more traditional sloyd (craft and design), have made Finnish technology education more diverse than in other Scandinavian countries.

In informal discussions among teachers and teacher educators, there seems to be a general feeling that technology education in Finnish primary schools is out of date, emphasising older technological processes such as the making of wooden and metal items. Even though technology education has been updated to an extent, there is a general feeling that there should be more connection to the modern technological world than that which exists presently.

The technological concepts of communication, construction, energy, manufacturing, and transportation are rarely reviewed from ecological, economical, cultural, and social viewpoints. The activities in which the pupils are engaged determine the kinds of technological knowledge and processes they learn. These activities must therefore be upgraded.

The Finnish comprehensive school provides compulsory basic education to pupils between the ages of 7 and 16. It is divided into a six-year lower level (grades 1-6), which corresponds internationally to primary education, and a three-year upper stage (grades 7-9), corresponding to lower secondary education.

In the third grade of the primary school, it is compulsory that all pupils study technology education. After that they have to choose either technology education or textile work. As one might expect, boys usually choose the former and girls choose the latter. Pupils who have chosen technology education study it for at least two hours a week from third through sixth grades.

In Finnish primary schools, technology education is usually taught by regular classroom teachers. Today these teachers must hold a master's degree in education and most have studied technology education as part of their teacher preparation program. A separate technology education room is provided for instruction, with an ideal maximum of 16 students in the facility at one a time.

The national curriculum reform in 1994 gave schools noticeably more freedom in developing their own curricula. The national core curriculum and curricular guidelines are very vague, providing only brief outlines. Though this allows for local flexibility, it also increases the diversity in the way in which technology education is taught from one school to another. In the latest national core curriculum, the main emphasis is on the "idea-to-product" process, with the pupil fully engaged in designing. Although, the designing and making of products remains as the central part of the national curriculum guidelines, the need for a broader technological understanding and capability is also mentioned.

The Finnish curriculum guidelines mention creativity, cultural heritage, environmental education, entrepreneur education, self-image, problem solving skills, social skills, and readiness for work life as the general goals of a comprehensive education. The responding teachers were asked to describe the extent to which pupils' activities in technology education corresponded to the goals.

Technology education focuses most on students' creativity. The development of problem-solving skills, self-image, cultural heritage, and social skills are also often associated with technology education. However, readiness for work life, environmental education, and entrepreneur education are associated to only a limited extent with technology education according to the responding teachers.

Traditional product design-based work includes the development of manual dexterity, product planning, work safety, work education, and aesthetic education.

The results indicated that manual dexterity was most central to the product design-based work. In addition, work education, work safety, and product planning were considered essential components. Aesthetics were considered to be a limited part of teaching and the pupils' work. It also included an assessment of the three dimensions of technological literacy as espoused by Dyrenfurth and Kozak and others: the utilisation of technology, the evaluation of technology, and the appreciation of technology. The utilisation of technology refers to the acquisition of the knowledge and skills necessary to use and make technological products and solutions. The evaluation of technology refers to the critical evaluation of the impact and consequences of technological processes. The appreciation of technology refers to understanding the outcomes of technological innovations as they relate to a higher standard of living.

One approach used in technology education involves students in the making of artifacts using prescribed drawings or plans. Pupils can also invent, design and make products by themselves. This second method is referred to as the "design teaching method." Five statements with a five-point scale focused on each teaching method. According to the results, the teachers use the design teaching method significantly more than the copying teaching method.

There are three most significant obstacles, in order, were:

i) Lack of financial resources.

ii) Insufficient material on how to teach technology education.

iii) Lack of other accompanying resources.

The lack of financial resources determines what type of teaching materials may be purchased. In turn, this relates to the teachers' perceptions about delivering a valid technology education program. One teacher, for example, stated, "Can anybody manage to develop technology education in a positive direction with these kinds of financial resources?" The lack of financial resources was followed by the lack of teaching ideas and the lack of other accompanying resources. The latter is related to classroom tools, machines, and other equipment that must be purchased with resources other than those used for supplies and materials. No significant differences among the respondents were found for the top three obstacles listed above. Though not at the top of the list, motivation was one of the obstacles identified. It was found that older teachers felt that they had significantly less motivation compared to younger teachers.

In short, the aim in developing technology education in primary schools is not to create a technology education classroom wherein pupils only read textbooks, watch videos, use computer software, and complete worksheets. The cultural, economic, natural, and social aspects, together with the technological aspects, should be considered in connection with designing and making products. Chemical and biotechnology could also be taught in conjunction with science, although they can also be taught in connection with design and making processes.

The history of technology could be correlated to humanities classes as well. In summary, the objects designed and made in technology education should not be "museum artifacts," but rather ones that are relevant to modern society. An example of such a project might be an electronic device found in some modern consumer product. In designing and making products, pupils should be taught to reflect upon the impact and consequences of technology to the society and the environment around them.

Technology Education in New Zealand

New Zealand is a small former British colony in the South Pacific with a population of 3.9 million people. The small economy of the country is heavily dependent on overseas trade. Historically, a large proportion of New Zealand's exports, mainly agricultural products, went to the United Kingdom. In the past 20 years, however, New Zealand has had to adapt to a changing world, so that now our largest exports are to Australia, Japan, the United States, and China.

New Zealand has, of necessity, moved away from its dependence on dairy, meat and wool exports, as the new industries of forestry, horticulture, fishing, manufacturing and tourism have become more significant. These changes, together with the huge advances in the associated technology, have created dramatic changes to our economy, and consequently, the fabric of New Zealand society.

There has been an increasing awareness of the delicate balance of our ecology, culture, economy and growth of a new independence. Major cultural changes, such as those that have resulted from our anti-nuclear stance, together with the re-emergence of a sense of identity within the indigenous Maori people, has resulted in the adoption of the Maori language an official language of the country. Along with this a unique New

Zealand identity and culture has developed. The result is that New Zealand has of necessity grown away from the traditional colonial influence of England. These words in the Anglican Book of Common Prayer are still true: "we are living in a new world...new knowledge and new ways of life bring with them new customs and forms of speech unknown before". Such changes have never been more explicit than in the field of technology, which has changed our ways, customs, and speech as no other aspect of daily life in New Zealand has.

The concept of technical education in New Zealand as it developed from the British model. It examines how England and Wales designed and introduced a new technology curriculum, and how, of necessity, a New Zealand technology curriculum has been developed which is more suited to New Zealand's developing culture. It illustrates some of the good features and some of the difficulties resulting from the introduction of technology as a subject in New Zealand schools in 1999.

The educational system of New Zealand, a former British colony, has understandably been influenced by the British school system. The public primary schooling system introduced in 1877 was made freely available to as many children as possible, and was "modelled on British and Australian counterparts". Until quite recently the New Zealand school system has been based on the three-term year, which was deliberately arranged around the New Zealand agricultural calendar, the breaks coinciding with:

— haymaking in January

— harvest/picking season in May

— lambing/calving in August

The late 19th century introduction of secondary schools to New Zealand was unashamedly academic. The secondary schools aligned themselves with the University of New Zealand by adopting the Matriculation Examination as an entrance requirement to University. According to Lee, "English thinking dominated schooling policy and practice in the young colony...secondary schools were inaccessible to most youth, particularly working class children". In 1901 a free place system was introduced in which every child was to be offered a free place in a secondary school. The tendency that followed was for most pupils to remain at secondary school for a short period only, while following an academic course.

The Minister of Lands in 1900 stated, "it was obviously the case in that children in the rural areas should be studying technical or agriculture subjects that would have a distinct bearing on the occupations in those localities".

As a result, by 1910 technical high schools had been established in the major centres throughout the country. This secondary school system now simulated the British tradition where middle class and academically strong went to a public or grammar school, and the working class went to a technical high school. (Although New Zealand society claims to be relatively classless by the British standards of family class structure, the division in any appearance of a New Zealand class structure is measured by an individual's wealth, rather than one's family connection).

As a typical example of this division in the early secondary education, the city of Hamilton is a small inland New Zealand city at the centre of one of the richest agricultural and pastoral areas in the world.

Hamilton had two secondary schools until the late 1950's, and prospective students were required take an entrance exam as a requirement to gain entry to Hamilton High School (HHS). The remaining students went to the Hamilton Technical College (HTC) for a technical (or pre-vocational) education. The Hamilton historian Gibbons described HTC as offering practical instruction for quite specific skills and careers, "to teach practical knowledge to the artisans and labourers of the future".

In the cities, New Zealand's technical high schools typically offered boys pre-vocational streams of engineering, building, or an agricultural course to give them a practical skill preparing them for the nonprofessional workforce. Academically less able female students were offered a commerce stream with subjects like typing and bookkeeping to prepare them for commerce, where it was expected that they would work, or alternatively as Gibbons described, "needlework, cooking and domestic economy". The small populations of the rural districts could not sustain a two-school system, and these post-primary schools, of necessity, continued to be mixed or comprehensive.

Such a system in these schools was now similar to the early British secondary school system on which ours was modelled. As described by Black "the major subject had hitherto been academic, with the vocational studies reserved for older students classed as less academically able". De Vries described a similar system in the Netherlands in which the courses were categorised as either "pre-vocational or pre-university".

The technical high school system, (or the technical streams in the comprehensive school), offered the students an education that they would otherwise perhaps not get. Gibbons pointed out that "in many ways hamilton residents were much more enthusiastic about the technical school than the ordinary high school...most adult Hamiltonians up to the 1920's had received little or no secondary education".

The Technical high school system had the following drawbacks:

i) Although a technical education was commonly thought to give the students who left school at the age of fifteen a useful start in industry, commerce, farming, or homemaking, it became increasingly so at the expense of a more rounded general and intellectual education. Within the British origin of a class system, this was never a concern in the British education system on which it was modelled.

ii) Pre-vocational courses were generally perceived (by parents and students) as for less able students, giving the subjects a low status, even if this was never the intention of a particular school offering the subjects. McKenzie observed "Inherited attitudes of the United Kingdom were an added handicap. In Britain, separate technical schools were typically associated in the public mind with second class knowledge which provided the limited skills and disciplined work habits of a docile working class". Similarly, the common fear of ambitious youth in New Zealand was that if they were directed into technical curricula, their vocational opportunities would be restricted.

iii) The system was sexist. The provision of a vocationally oriented education in reality, as O'Neil subtly put it, "meant the formalised entrenchment of gender differentiated (practical) vocational courses...male pupils took vocational courses for their future paid employment, some females took them for theirs, but many did so in the light of their expected future in unpaid domestic labour".

By the 1930s, there was a strong case to dispense with the two types of school, and thereby dispense with the associated class attitudes. In 1945 the Department of Education imposed a common core curriculum on all types of schools. This did not inhibit the ambitions of the academics or frustrate the aspirations of the ambitious, but it ensured a common range of studies, including craft subjects for the junior pupils. Students at post primary schools were able to take technical subjects, including workshop craft subjects. While this education system and its crafts may have been appropriate for earlier times, in more recent years it has generated the following problems:

— Frequently, the technology learned in schools did not help students in society because the equipment they used was often industrial or commercial cast-off and therefore likely to be obsolete and out-of-date.
— The school environment can be unrealistic and lack an examination of the social issues of technology.
— There is nothing wrong with craft skills themselves as an element in education. The problem with traditional craft teaching‹woodwork, for example‹as an educational endeavour has rather been that the disciplines are learned within a context that limits their general applicability to build a coffee table in school is to learn not a generalised competence capable of application anywhere but a competence for one context, school.

— The teaching of technical subjects requires skilled teaching staff. The separate technical and craft learning activities in New Zealand tended to be isolated from each other. The technological knowledge areas were not linked in a structured manner in which the knowledge could transfer from one situation to another.

— The curriculum did not encourage team working. In today's work environment it is likely that a professional will have to work in a group relationship to solve a problem or operate a system. ral individuals whose work must be coordinated".

— The curriculum was not considered responsive to New Zealand's particular needs, languages, and cultural differences.

Although New Zealand has this long history of technical education in the intermediate and secondary schools, the delivery of general secondary school education has not always related the students to a realistic social framework of knowledge which is applicable to an increasingly technological world. What is required is a technical education system for all students. However, unlike the traditional technology programs, which formerly taught only skill-based programs, the technology instruction in schools must change to meet the needs of a technologically advanced society. Johnson asked the question, "given the fact that the skills needed by the workforce are changing and the increased need for all citizens to have high level thinking skills, are the students being provided the opportunity to acquire those skills?".

New Zealand underwent major curriculum reforms in the 1990's The development of a national curriculum was part of this reform. This resulted from growing concerns with school curriculum. During the 1970s and 1980s, calls were made for a curriculum that was responsive to New Zealand's needs for people highly skilled in science and technology, and with the languagc and cultural sensitivity needed to maintain international economic competitiveness. Technology subjects need to be accessible to all children, regardless of gender or social standing. Along this line, Black and Harrison proffered the general idea of technological capability with a task-action-capability (TAC) approach. They listed three interacting personal attributes required in the education of children to be of direct practical value in the real world:

— "Resources of knowledge, skill and experience which can be drawn upon, consciously or subconsciously, when involved in active tasks.

— *Capability* to perform, to originate, to get things done, to stand by decisions.

— *Awareness*, perception and understanding needed for making balanced and effective value judgement"

The Government of New Zealand undertook a revision of curriculum in 1990 under the banner of *The Achievement Initiative*. The object was to explore ideas influenced by the curriculum reforms that were taking place in England and Wales. A Ministerial Task Group Reviewing Science and Technology Education was set up in 1991 which made many recommendations, the most significant being that a technology curriculum be developed as an area in its own right. The report recommended a technological education for all students, to develop people who are creative, innovative, and resourceful and who can combine enterprise, initiative, and imagination with knowledge and skills. The report went even further in its recommendations to include:

i) the importance of teaching and assessing interpersonal, communication and broadly-based practical skills;

ii) a broad range of knowledge and skills recognised by assessment procedures;

iii) adequate teacher training and resourcing for technology education;

iv) Maori input and inclusion of the use of Maori language.

Within a range of technological areas and contexts, students should develop and understanding of:

1. The use and operation of technologies;
2. Technological principles and systems;
3. The nature of technological practice;
4. Strategies for the communication, promotion, and evaluation of technological ideas and outcomes.

Within a range of technological areas and contexts, students should produce technological solutions. They will:

5. Identify needs and opportunities to provide information for possible technological practice;
6. With reference to identified needs and opportunities,
   (a) generate possible options and strategies, and select, develop and adapt appropriate solutions;
   (b) produce technological outcomes to agreed quality standards, managing time, using human and physical resources skillfully, safely and effectively;

(c) present and promote ideas, strategies, and outcomes throughout technological practice;

(d) evaluate designs, strategies, and outcomes throughout technological practice in relation to their own activities and those of others.

Within a range of technological areas and contexts, students should:

7. Develop awareness and understanding of the beliefs, values, and ethics of individuals and groups:

   (a) promote or constrain technological development;

   (b) influence attitudes towards technological development;

8. Develop awareness and understanding of the impacts of technology on society and the environment:

   (a) in the past, present and possible future;

   (b) in local, national and international settings.

The curriculum is a multi-layered structure. Each of these three strands has 8 levels of itemised achievement objectives, to serve the subject as the children progress through the school system over a period of 13 years .

The New Zealand technology curriculum is the result of a group of experienced curriculum writers, some of whom had experience in rewriting the science and mathematics curriculums. The development policy was a result of the wider community input and also a result of much international research into technical education, teaching, and learning.

The New Zealand curriculum is not simply the copy of an overseas model with a few wording changes. It is a break from the British modelling of the past, with a new subject that is reflective of New Zealand conditions and culture, and with a knowledge base of its own which incorporates a balance of intellectual, social, and personal interactions with technology. The curriculum appears to be well balanced. It is not a fragmented assemblage that tries to cobble together a whole spectrum of existing subjects and crafts. The design may be varied to suit particular areas of the country and it is also versatile enough to reflect current technological practices.

It may be difficult for the technology curriculum to succeed until it has full status, equal to other subjects in the school curriculum. In the transition stage there are potential problems in the successful introduction:

a) As McCormick had observed with the prototype England and Wales technology curriculum, many of the original technical/craft subcultures do not naturally work together. The former areas of arts and crafts that were rather specialised are now merged into a new curriculum where technology teachers are no longer required to be expert in a very narrow field of technology. Most of the nontechnical teachers will initially lack the appropriate technological expertise. Similarly, the former specialised subject teachers will now require more general knowledge and skills in technology and education. The recommendation of the Ministry of Research, Science, and Technology to provide for adequate training and resourcing must be taken very seriously.

b) It follows from the above that the teachers will not always have the answers and must of necessity change their roles to mentors and facilitators. While the successful teaching of the subject will encourage talking, the exchange of ideas, questioning, and curiosity which is excellent for the development of group dynamics, some children's cultures do not encourage it. Moli observed of the Polynesian immigrants into New Zealand that "...many have learned from parents that the teacher, like the priest or pastor, holds valuable knowledge and as such is to be respected, not questioned by mere students. Indeed, to ask a question can be a sign of lack of attention and disrespect. ...to teach the children to be critical thinkers and to ask questions in an inquiry approach is certainly opposing the conforming aspects of the culture". It is not a problem just for one culture in our multicultural New Zealand schools and society.

c) The standard New Zealand primary classrooms do not have facilities to out carry some of the curriculum projects.

d) The development and implementation of the subject can easily be undermined by misinterpretation.

To solve these problems, and successfully implement the technology curriculum, the teaching of technology as we have known it in the past will change. Vincent and Vincent stated that "curriculum change may denote bringing about changes in methods of teaching and learning, as well as changes in the programmes or courses". The curriculum states that a timetable for the subject of technology "allows for teachers to work collaboratively in planning and delivery". Effective planning of the subject necessitates an increase in the number of meetings the teachers must attend which, in turn, has increased their workload. Recognition of this problem has resulted in a reduced requirement for teaching technology in the first year of the programme's implementation. A gradual phasing in of the subject resulted in a partial implementation of years 7-8 and 9-10 in 1999.

Technological knowledge is increasing at an exponential rate and the professionals of today work in environments where they can no longer be expected to learn in advance all the technological knowledge required to solve day-to-day problems. Knowledge must constantly be acquired in order to understand technology and solve the problems of the time. It is difficult to train a person for a professional situation where the demands of tasks may be to some extent unpredictable, and where the knowledge and skills needed are not usually defined by some prior instruction or coaching of the concept or process. McCormick stated: "Technological activity is by nature multidimensional, requiring understanding from a variety of points of view". In addition, most people working in a technological occupation must retrain in technology at least once in their working lifetime.

As this knowledge explosion continues, the balance between *what to learn* and *how to learn* must shift towards the latter. Given the impossibility of knowing everything about anything, the educational requirements for a job and those for higher education are converging. The Carnegie Task Force observed that "...the economic and social needs of our country will force us to provide for many the kind of education previously reserved for the elite few". Vincent and Vincent go even further and stated that "Oral and social skills, it is argued, are the skills most employers need from their employees".

New Zealand education has taken positive steps to define and establish technology education as an academic discipline to replace traditional school craft subjects. All students are expected to study technology following a structured progression of the curriculum from their first year in primary school to their senior secondary year 13. The success of the technology curriculum will depend upon its successful implementation in the schools, together with the development of an effective assessment program. Naturally it will take time to develop a culture of technology education in New Zealand schools, as "...technology education does not have a historical home in New Zealand". The exams that students sit in the 7th form (the final secondary school year required as a university entrance qualification) are the exams that possess social status. It can be expected that the subject of technology will gain an appropriate social status and break its current shackles as a pre-vocational course when it eventually becomes a 7th Form exam.

The examination unit standards for the subject are currently being written and will be phased in gradually, starting in 2001. A panel of academic professionals is developing the achievement standards, professional development requirements, and resources for year eleven and will be introduced in 2000.

Unlike the old pre-vocation training in the technical schools, the new subject of technology will be of assistance in acquainting the New Zealand pupils with the aspects of technology that are important in the 21st century. It will provide students with the knowledge and skills that will be useful, regardless of the career path they choose, by increasing their options, horizons, and perspectives).

The process that resulted in Technology in the New Zealand Curriculum was designed to give the students an understanding of the culture, the values, and the social issues involved with technology. It is intended to bring the concept of technological literacy into the intellectual domain. Such an understanding and intellectual approach to technology is now deemed necessary for all students in order for them to function effectively in our modern technological society. The new subject will lay a good foundation for further technological learning in school as well as the inevitable learning that takes place outside the school in the home and at work.

Nickerson went even further in expressing the view that technology education will "...increase one's appreciation of other cultures, viewpoints and lifestyles, and deepen one's sensitivities to other people's rights, feelings, preferences and hopes...it should heighten one's curiosity and inquisitiveness; as a consequence of one[1]s education, the world should be a far more interesting place than it would otherwise be".

Creative productivity in Technology Education

The creative product embodies the very essence of technology. The American Association for the Advancement of Science stated, "Technology is best described as a process, but is most commonly known by its products and their effects on society". A product can be described as a physical object, article, patent, theoretical system, an equation, or new technique. A creative product is one that possesses some degree of unusualness (originality) and usefulness. When given the opportunity for self-expression, a student's project becomes nothing less than a creative product.

The creative product can be viewed as a physical representation of a person's "true" creative ability encapsulating both the creative person and process. By examining the literature related to the creative person and process, technology educators may gain a deeper understanding of the creative product itself.

Inventors such as Edison and Ford have been recognised as being highly creative. Why some people reach a level of creative genius while others do not is still unknown. However, Maslow, after studying several of his subjects, determined that all people are creative, not in the sense of creating great works, but rather, creative in a universal sense that attributes a portion of creative talent to every person. In trying to understand and predict a person's creative ability, two factors have often been considered: intelligence and personality.

A frequently asked question among educators is "What is the relationship between creativity and intelligence?" Research has shown that there is no direct correlation between creativity and intelligence quotient (I.Q.). Edmunds conducted a study to determine whether there was a relationship between creativity and I.Q. Two hundred and eighty-one randomly selected students, grades eight to eleven, from three different schools in New Brunswick, Canada participated.

The instruments used to collect data were the Torrance Test of Creative Thinking and the Otis-Lennon School Ability Test, used to test intellectual ability. Based on a Pearson product moment analysis, results showed that I.Q. scores did not significantly correlate with creativity scores. The findings were consistent with the literature dealing with creativity and intelligence.

On a practical level, findings similar to the one above may explain why I.Q. measures have proven to be unsuccessful in predicting creative performance. Hayes pointed out that creative performance may be better predicted by isolating and investigating personality traits.

Researchers have shown that there are certain personality traits associated with creative people. Runco, Nemiro, and Walberg identified and conducted a survey investigating personality traits associated with the creative person. The survey was mailed to 400 individuals who had submitted papers and/or published articles related to creativity. The researchers asked participants to rate, in order of importance, various traits that they believed affected creative achievement.

The survey contained 16 creative achievement clusters consisting of 141 items. One hundred and forty-three surveys were returned reflecting a response of 35.8%. Results demonstrated that intrinsic motivation, problem finding, and questioning skills were considered the most important traits in predicting and identifying creative achievement. Though personality traits play an important part in understanding creative ability, an equally important area of creativity theory lies in the identification of the creative process itself.

Creativity is a process that has been represented using various models. Wallas offered one of the earliest explanations of the creative process. His model consisted of four stages that are briefly described below:

i) *Preparation*: This is the first stage in which an individual identifies then investigates a problem from many different angles.

ii) *Incubation:* At this stage the individual stops all conscious work related to the problem.

iii) *Illumination*: This stage is characterised by a sudden or immediate solution to the problem.

iv) *Verification*: This is the last stage at which time the solution is tested.

Wallas' model has served as a foundation upon which other models have been built. Some researchers have added the communication stage to the creative process. The communication stage is the final stage of the creative process. At this stage, the new idea confined to one's mind is transformed into a verbal or nonverbal product. The product is then shared within a social context in order that others may react to and possibly accept or reject it. A more comprehensive description of the creative process is captured within a definition offered by Torrance.

Creativity is a process of becoming sensitive to problems, deficiencies, gaps in knowledge, missing elements, disharmonies, and so on; identifying the difficult; searching for solutions, making guesses or formulating hypotheses about the deficiencies, testing and re-testing these hypotheses and possibly modifying and re-testing them, and finally communicating the results. Torrance's definition resembles what some have referred to as problem solving. For example, technology educators Savage and Sterry, generalising from the work of several scholars, identified six steps to the problem-solving process:

i) *Defining the problem*: Analysing, gathering information, and establishing limitations that will isolate and identify the need or opportunity.

ii) *Developing alternative solutions*: Using principles, ideation, and brainstorming to develop alternate ways to meet the opportunity or solve the problem.

iii) *Selecting a solution*: Selecting the most plausible solution by identifying, modifying, and/or combining ideas from the group of possible solutions.

iv) *Implementing and evaluating the solution*: Modelling, operating, and assessing the effectiveness of the selected solution.

v) *Redesigning the solution*: Incorporating improvements into the design of the solution that address needs identified during the evaluation phase.

vi) *Interpreting the solution*: Synthesising and communicating the characteristics and operating parameters of the solution.

By closely comparing Torrance's definition of creativity with that of Savage and Sterry's problem solving process, one can easily see similarities between the descriptions. Guilford, a leading expert in the study of creativity, made a similar comparison between steps of the creative process offered by Wallas with those of the problem solving process proposed by the noted educational philosopher, John Dewey. In doing so, Guilford simply concluded that, "Problem-solving is creative; there is no other kind".

Hinton combined the creative process and problem solving process into what is now known as creative problem solving. He believed that creativity would be better understood if placed within a problem solving structure. Creative problem solving is a subset of problem- solving based on the assumption that not all problems require a creative solution. He surmised that when a problem is solved with a learned response, then no creativity has been expressed. However, when a simple problem is solved with an insightful response, then a small measure of creativity has been expressed, when a complex problem is solved with a novel solution, then genuine creativity has occurred.

Genuine creativity is the result of the creative process that manifests itself into a creative product. Understanding the creative process as well as the creative person may play an important role in realising the true nature of the creative product. Though researchers have not reached a consensus as to what attributes make up the creative product, identifying and evaluating the creative product has been a concern of some researchers.

Moss and Duenk have arguably conducted the most extensive research establishing criteria for evaluating creative products within industrial arts/technology education. Moss, in examining the criterion problem, concluded that unusualness (originality) and usefulness were the defining characteristics of the creative product produced by industrial arts students. A description of his model is presented below:

- *Unusualness*: To be creative a product must possess some degree of unusualness [or originality]. The quality of unusualness may, theoretically, be measured in terms of probability of occurrence; the less the probability of its occurrence, the more unusual the product.
- *Usefulness*: While some degree of unusualness is a necessary requirement for creative products, it is not a sufficient condition. To be creative, an industrial arts student's product must also satisfy the minimal

principle requirements of the problem situation; to some degree it must "work" or be potentially "workable." Completely ineffective, irrelevant solutions to teacher-imposed or student-initiated problems are not creative.

— *Combining Unusualness and Usefulness*: When a product possesses some degree of both unusualness and usefulness, it is creative. But, because these two criterion qualities are considered variables, the degree of creativity among products will also vary. The extent of each product's departure from the typical and its value as a problem solution will, in combination, determine the degree of creativity of each product. Giving the two qualities equal weight, as the unusualness and/or usefulness of a product increases so does its rated creativity; similarly, as the product approaches the conventional and/or uselessness its rated creativity decreases.

In establishing the construct validity of his theoretical model, Moss submitted his work for review to 57 industrial arts educators, two measurement specialists, and six educational psychologists. Results of the review found the proposed model was compatible with existing theory and practice of both creativity and industrial arts. No one disagreed with the major premise of using unusualness and usefulness as defining characteristics for evaluating the creative products of industrial arts students.

To date, little additional research has been conducted to establish criteria for evaluating the creative products of industrial arts and/or technology education students. If technology is best known by its creative products, then technology educators are obligated to identify characteristics that make a product more or less creative.

Furthermore, educators must find ways to objectively measure these attributes and then teach students in a manner that enhances the creativity of their products. A possible approach to enhancing product creativity is by incorporating computer simulation technology into the classroom. However, no research has been done in this area to measure the true effect of computer simulation on product creativity. For that reason, other studies addressing computer use in general and product creativity will be explored.

A study conducted by Joram, Woodruff, Bryson, & Lindsay found that average students produced their most creative work using word processors as compared to students using pencil and paper. The researchers hypothesised that word-processing would hinder product creativity due to constant evaluation and editing of their work. To test the hypotheses, average and above average eighth grade writers were randomly assigned to one of two groups. The first group was asked to compose using word processors while the second group was asked to compose using pencil and paper. After collecting the compositions, both the word-processed and handwritten texts were typed so that they would be in the same format for the evaluators. Based on the results, the researchers concluded that word-processing enhances the creative abilities of average writers.

The researchers attributed this to the prospect that word-processing may allow the average writer to generate a number of ideas, knowing that only a few of them will be usable and the rest can be easily erased. However, the researchers also found that word-processing had a negative effect on the creativity of above average writers. These mixed results suggest that the use of word-processing may not be appropriate for all students relative to creativity.

Similar to word processing, computer graphic programs may also help students improve the creativeness of their products. In a study conducted by Howe, two advanced undergraduate classes in graphic design were assigned to one of two treatments. The first treatment group was instructed to use a computer graphic program to complete a design project whereas the other group was asked to use conventional graphic design equipment to design their product.

Upon completion of the assignment, both groups' projects were collected and photocopied so that they would be in the same format before being evaluated. Based on the results, the researcher concluded that students using computer graphics technology surpassed the conventional method in product creativity. The researchers attributed this to the prospect that computer graphics programs may enable graphic designers to generate an abundance of ideas, then capture the most creative ones and incorporate them into their designs. However, due to a lack of random assignment, results of the study should be generalised with caution.

Like word processing and computer graphics, simulation technology is a type of computer application that allows users to freely manipulate and edit virtual objects. Thus it was surmised that computer simulation may enhance creativity.

Some researchers believe that computers in general may improve student product creativity by allowing students to generate an abundance of ideas, capture the most creative ones, and incorporate them into their product. Similarly, some researchers speculate that the use of computer simulations may enhance product creativity as well. However, based on the results of this study, the use of computer simulation to enhance product creativity was not supported. The creativity, usefulness, or originality of the resulting products appears to be the same whether students use a computer simulation of Lego blocks or whether they manipulated the actual blocks.

When studying a computer simulation's effect on student product creativity, researchers may want to focus more attention on the creative person's traits and the cognitive process used to create the product rather than focusing on the tool or means by which the product was created. This approach to understanding student product creativity may lend itself more to qualitative rather than quantitative research. If quantitative research is to continue in this area of study, researchers may wish to consider using a different theoretical model and instrument for measuring the creative product.

For example, if replicating this experiment, rather than using only the two sub-scales of the Creative Product Semantic Scale, the complete instrument might be used, yielding additional dimensions of creativity. Additional research regarding the various types of simulation programs is needed, along with the different effects they might have on student creativity in designing products. The use of computer simulations in technology education programs appears to be increasing with little research to support their effectiveness or viable use.

CHAPTER 6

Technology Education for All

Technology, and certainly technology education, can be characterised as more of an activity than a discrete body of content. Technological knowledge can be divided into procedural knowledge which relates to the activity, and conceptual knowledge which relates to the body of content. There is probably more international agreement among technology educators about the activity of technology than about the content of technology. This is a helpful separation to make when designing curriculum and discussing teaching, but it is not a separation which should be evident to the students.

Students should perceive technology as a thoroughly integrated activity, not one which can be separated into content and process, or theory and practice. Some curriculum documents separate these two areas of knowledge. An example is the two attainment targets in the UK technology curriculum of Design and Make. In others, the differentiation is less such as the Content Standards of the Technology for all Americans Project. While the traditional focus of technology education has been on activity, i.e., on doing and making things, this has represented a narrow interpretation of procedural knowledge. This focus has not been accompanied by an emphasis on all aspects of procedural knowledge, but has typically been concerned with those procedures most closely aligned with the development of manipulative skills and how to use tools effectively and safely, for example.

A relatively recent realisation has been that there are many significant cognitive skills which areimportant for students to develop, and which are suitable to be developed in the unique context of technology education. The term unique is appropriate because there is no other curriculum area in which students have as significant an opportunity to think and reflect and develop ideas, and then to test their ideas in a practical context. The development of these cognitive skills occurs through the procedural knowledge of technology education.

Procedural knowledge is developed through the creation of a process, as when a solution to a particular need or brief is sought. There are a range of these processes which are utilised in the development of technology and therefore may also be appropriate in teaching technology, the two most common being design and problem solving.

The place of procedural knowledge in the US Standards for Technology Education is developed as "Design," proposed as one of the five major organisers of technology education. This equation of the technological process with design is further reinforced by another of the organisers, namely "The Designed World."

A common approach in teaching the technology process is to map out a series of steps for students to follow as they make projects. Examples include design-make-appraise, identify-design-make-evaluate (UK Department of Education, 1995), and define problem-ideas-model-test. The idea is that this systematic process can be taught and learned by all pupils who can then apply it to subsequent problems or situations. These are often reproduced in booklet form as workbooks for students to use as they design.

However, research has revealed that it does not work this way, either in reality or in the classroom. Neither students nor designers naturally utilise a predetermined process in their work; they invent a process as they proceed toward task completion. This is well illustrated by Petroski in his book Invention by Design where he details the design and development of things like paper clips, pencil points, and zippers.

The parallels with science education are interesting. As with technology, and even more specifically with design in technology, studies of scientists at work seem to indicate that there is no generalisable method. The notion that there is a common series of steps followed by all research scientists, such as defining the problem, gathering information, forming a hypothesis, making observations, testing hypotheses, and drawing conclusions, is not generally held.

One of the reasons for the continued perpetration of this myth is the way in which results are presented in research journals. The standardised style of presentation makes it appear that all scientists follow a standard research plan. Scientists approach and solve problems in many different ways, using the skills and methods used by all problem solvers in whatever area.

Process of Technology Education

There is a range of activities in which students are engaged when they "do" technology. They do not necessarily do all the activities every time they complete a task, and certainly do not do them in the same order every time. The activities depend on the nature of the student and the nature of the problem. There are many activities in this process, but the most important include:

— evaluation,

— communication,

— modelling,

— generating ideas,

— research and investigation,

— producing

— documenting.

It may be appropriate that these activities be called aspects rather than stages of the process; stages has sequential connotation which is not appropriate as a technology process.

If these aspects are standardised and sequenced for all students for all projects, then it is not possible to achieve the goal of revealing the cognitive development of students through the documentation of their design process. This is the case because they are being forced into a way of thinking that has been predetermined by the teacher.

Their cognitive development is neither revealed nor encouraged. These activities are not ends in themselves, but rather are done and practised in order to achieve other goals. These other goals include students becoming independent problem solvers, becoming creative and reflective, and becoming critical and expressive; that is, the goals are achievement of the generic competencies that all students need and should have upon leaving school.

The situation in Western Australia is representative of more global thinking about the nature of the processes of technology. There has been a move away from the notion of a prescribed process such as Design-Make-Appraise to the idea that there is a range of processes in which students are engaged when they do technology. These processes of technology may include those enumerated in the following section.

Design

Design is justifiably the most common and popular of the processes appropriate to technology education, and has been identified as such in the US Standards for Technology Education. In the real world it is a significant process in the development of technology in many disciplines from engineering to architecture, and from an educational perspective it is an ideal methodology to use as a vehicle to achieve the desired competencies. There is very little research about design, and therefore very little informed guidance on how to teach it. But there is some. There seems to be no simple generalisable process. "The processes involved in designing are not linear, they do not always start from human needs, and they do not always proceed in an orderly way. They are reiterative, spiralling back on themselves, proceeding by incremental change and occasional flashes of insight".

Research has been conducted on both expert designers and children doing design in a technology education context with some parallels in the findings. What students do when they design in technology is a very convoluted and complex process, and is different every time they design something.

Studies of designers working in technological fields also reject the notion that what they do can be represented by an algorithm. So both seem to adopt inventive and flexible approaches which are adapted to the situation in which they are working. Individuals also seem to have preferences for how they design.

In the design situation where teachers insist on progressing through set stages, students in fact adopt their own strategies in order to get the job done, but ritualistically use the teacher's approach to satisfy assessment demands. For example in the common requirement to sketch four design alternatives to a problem or brief, a student is often interested in only one, and does the others just to satisfy the teacher. In this case the goal of generating creative ideas is not being achieved and students do not reflect on the process, for example, by asking what, why, what order? This requirement therefore has no impact on student thinking or the development of creativity.

Problem Solving

The appeal of problem solving as a methodology lies in the fact that it is a natural activity; humans have always been faced with problems and tried to solve them. In this sense it is also a useful model for understanding technological development in that it can incorporate the broad range of variables involved in the solution to a technological problem.

Despite the fact that the terms design and problem solving are often used interchangeably, problem solving is different from design in that design deals with ill defined problems and may not begin with a problem, while of course problem solving does. It is helpful to clarify different types of problem solving. McCormick identified three types of problem solving:

i) a general problem solving approach referring to the process more than the problem itself.

ii) a global problem referring to a significant problem, the solution to which will take some time.

iii) emergent problems which arise throughout any process and must be overcome in order to proceed.

Systems Approach

A systems approach (input-process-output) is often placed in a problem solving context. For example, in many technology curricula in the USA a system is represented as a solution to a problem. A systems approach may be either analytical, and thereby used as a way of viewing the world or a specific context or object, or functional in that a systems process is followed for diagnostic or production purposes.

Many generic groups of systems are represented in the literature. Examples include structural, mechanical, electronic, communication, production, transportation and biotechnological systems. These systems represent much of technology, and are often used to reduce a technology to a simple graphic model that illustrates basic elements. This representation can extend to quite complex elements such as systems maps, influence diagrams, and flow-block diagrams.

Invention

Inventions may be accidental or intentional. Authors such as Ferre equate the accidental with the notion of practical intelligence in technology, the "trial and error" and "all or nothing" approaches. The intentional is conversely associated with theoretical intelligence, where each element contributing toward a technological solution can be isolated and analysed for its effectiveness. A method can be articulated, aligned with the notion of theoretical intelligence in technology, which represents a systematic and deliberate process for the pursuit of new inventions.

To the extent that this is a realistic process, invention can be encouraged in the classroom. A deeper discussion of the psychology of invention would be necessary to ascertain if the characteristic of invention itself can be taught. But generally speaking, a classroom climate, and an understanding of what constitutes a technology process can both be conducive to the acceptance of invention when it occurs in a classroom.

Manufacturing

A manufacturing orientation to technology covers a number of more specific types of processes such as a custom made craft approach, a production line, batch production, and one-off production. In each of these processes, factors to consider include materials, capital, information, transportation, time, and energy. This is an accepted feature of many technology education programs, and continues to be justified because it is an important aspect of real-world technology. There are many other processes that are used in various technological contexts and could be used by teachers to help represent the breadth of technology to students. For example, repair and restoration, or the development of a business plan, could each be a valid process.

Teaching of Processes

The variety in pedagogy afforded by the utilisation of a range of processes has a number of potential advantages:

— appeals to the preferred learning styles of a range of learners
— makes both teaching and learning more interesting
— more adequately reflects technology

The difficulty in teaching these processes of technology becomes apparent when students are not all doing the same activity at the same time. This means that the students in a class cannot be treated the same as far as teacher attention is concerned. Despite the fact that all students may be working on the same problem, they may be utilising different processes in seeking a solution, and aiming toward different solutions. Thus, the demands for guidance from the teacher vary. The following are some anecdotal ideas to deal with this situation.

1. Begin with a large group.

In this approach, a situation, problem, or brief is presented and discussed with a class. Then, consensus agreement is reached on a procedural sequence through discussion by class members. After agreement about the approach has been achieved, the teacher can then put a label on each of the activities. For example, "when we looked at similar products on the market, we were evaluating," or "when you asked your friends and neighbours how much they would pay for the product, we were doing market research." The determination of the process is not then dependent on an individual and students begin with the necessity of the activity rather than the possibly meaningless label that goes with it.

2. Don't expect too much too soon from students.

Because the skills involved in technology processes are complex and convoluted, and are different each time a solution to a problem is attempted, it will take a long time to teach the various aspects of processes. It will require even more time for students to practice using those processes selectively and effectively. Lower secondary students should not be expected to proceed individually through a sound and comprehensive self directed technology process. It is not until the upper secondary level that this should be expected to take place.

3. New conceptual and procedural knowledge.

New knowledge must be taught on a need-to-know basis. It is not good enough to tell the students that "teacher knows best, and while the material currently seems irrelevant, there will come a time when it is needed." Because the processes are complex, they should be taught bits at a time. The skill (and most difficult part) of teaching technology is to manipulate students to the point where they realise they need the information you want them to have. The situation should not arise where technology students are stuck in a classroom for the first few weeks of a course because of all the information they need to have in order, for example for them to be able to do design. This will destroy their motivation and enthusiasm for the subject. If students are given information when they realise they need it, their level of retention is higher and they will learn more efficiently.

4. Large projects which last for an extended period of time.

When the students are involved in large projects which last for a period of time, introduce smaller support tasks to give practice in specific skills which can then be immediately applied to the context of the task in which they are working. For example shorter tasks could include the development of a particular graphics skill, practice in identifying peoples' needs, or the identification or manipulation of systems.

5. Minimise the separation of theory and practice.

The continual interaction between the thinking skills and the concrete reality of activity is what enables the development of capability in technology. But often and in many ways we indicate to students that these two areas are discrete. This separation is evident in:

i) timetabling - theory and practical sessions scheduled at different times

ii) examinations - separate theory and practical exams

iii) the use and design of work spaces - theory areas and practical areas

iv) teaching methods - lecturing versus demonstrations.

Students should get the clear message, both through overt and covert strategies, that theory and thinking in technology cannot be separated from technological activity. Either without the other is not representing technology adequately to students.

6. The process can begin at different places.

The point at which the process begins will depend on the outcomes the teacher wishes the students to achieve. It may begin with:

— exposure to a situation, from which students extract a problem,

— a description of the problem,

— a brief already written by the teacher,

— an individual and predefined interest or need,

— an existing product, which is then evaluated for redesign.

7. Support the required skills.

Students must be taught, and then given the opportunities to practice specific skills and techniques before expecting them to incorporate them into a process of technology. Most technology teachers do this well in the area of manipulative skills, but it is also essential for the cognitive skills. For example if we want students to generate ideas, then we need to teach them the skills of brainstorming and morphological analyses. In researching they must be taught survey design or how to use indexes. Specific sketching skills must be taught for them to be able to record ideas. If metacognition is expected, then they need to understand how they think.

8. The sequence of the process.

The point at which the process is initiated may dictate the beginning of the sequence of activities. For example, if a product is to be examined for redesign, then evaluation occurs first; if the activity results from personal need, then the generation of creative ideas may not be necessary. It may be appropriate to prototype ideas early in the process, then go back and revise the brief. As previously stated, there is no set process.

9. The end result of the process may vary.

The most common end result of a design process is a product, but it could just as appropriately be a model or prototype, environment, graphic, system, or service. If a course of study in technology always results in one type of output, there is a danger that the student will develop a limited perception of the nature of technology.

Technology is such a broad area that a focus on any one process will not provide students with a broad concept of the nature of technology. All students have preferred learning styles, and utilising a range of processes in teaching technology will appeal to more students than would the use of a single process. It will also make the teaching of technology more interesting to both students and teachers.

Motivation of Technology Teachres

Technology education has undergone radical changes over the past decade. The content, instructional methodologies, and facilities are among the key indicators of change as is the background and motivation of people who choose to become technology teachers. Individuals interested in computers and electronic communication are seeking technology teaching positions, as contrasted with interests in woodworking and metalworking that typified the past.

The profession could benefit from information about how these changes have affected teachers' enjoyment of teaching. This information could inform the process of recruiting new teachers by better understanding the rewards and stresses associated with major programmatic change. What is it about the current teaching climate in technology education that outstanding teachers find most rewarding?

Technology education is having difficulty recruiting talented teachers. Current estimates place the number of job openings at six or more for each technology education baccalaureate graduate. Attractive salary and benefit packages accompany many of these openings. Why is it so difficult to attract and retain talented technology teachers? What is it about teaching technology education that makes outstanding teachers love their jobs?

In conjunction with an ITEA task force, a study was conducted to determine the factors associated with college students' decision to select technology teaching as a career. This research was designed to provide an information base for subsequent recruitment efforts. Another responsibility of the Task Force was to identify the specific aspects of teaching that outstanding, nationally-recognised technology education teachers find to be particularly rewarding and most distressing. Another goal was to obtain suggestions about changes necessary to make their jobs more enjoyable.

During the first half of the 20th century, job satisfaction was viewed as a continuum. Certain factors, if present, contributed to job satisfaction; if absent, they contributed to job dissatisfaction. In contrast, Herzberg, Mausner, and Snyderman developed the Two-Factor Theory of job satisfaction, also called the Motivation-Hygiene Theory. They concluded that there were specific conditions of employment that are job satisfiers (motivators), while other conditions act as job dissatisfiers (hygiene factors).

Research has established a relationship between teacher satisfaction and student achievement. The findings indicate that secondary school teacher morale depends in part on whether their students were relatively high scholastic achievers. Similarly, student achievement tended to increase as a function of high teacher morale. Teacher morale or satisfaction may be one of the most important factors affecting student achievement, and therefore, is a critical topic to be researched. The literature on teacher satisfaction indicates that job satisfaction is the result of many interrelated factors.

Studies of teacher satisfaction based on Maslow's hierarchy of needs theory have supported the connection between need-fulfilment and job satisfaction. These authors cited an absence of three higher-order needs (esteem, autonomy, and self-actualisation) as major contributors to low teacher satisfaction. Simmons has identified teacher satisfaction factors and has categorised them as *content* and *context*. Content factors relate to the teaching process itself (e.g., achievement in teaching, the nature of the work itself, and recognition), while context factors relate to the job situation (e.g., interpersonal relations, school policy, salary, etc.). The context serves only to reduce pain in the lower-order needs areas (e.g., physiological and safety) and cannot lead to satisfaction. The content aspects correspond to esteem and self-actualisation, which are at the top of Maslow's hierarchy. Those factors that are *content*-centered (i.e., intrinsic aspects of teaching) contribute most powerfully to satisfaction.

According to a recent national survey (USDOE, 1992), approximately 32% of new teachers chose the teaching profession because they enjoy working with children. Approximately 30% found the teaching process satisfying. The same report projected that the number of teachers would need to increase from 2.8 million in 1991 to 3.3 million in 2002 to meet the demand.

Clarke and Keating discovered that interaction with students was the most satisfying aspect for teachers, while lack of administrative support was the least satisfying aspect. Perkins observed that teacher satisfaction was not significantly affected by background variables such as teacher or principal gender, years of experience, or school-type assignment. Perkins also found that teachers are most satisfied with their co-workers and least satisfied with the monetary aspects of teaching. Inadequate salary, low status of the profession, and excessive paperwork are some common sources of distress that affect job satisfaction.

Teachers' perception of locus of control is another factor influencing job satisfaction. Bein, Anderson, and Maes found a negative correlation between job satisfaction and teachers' perceptions of external control. Those with a greater sense of personal control were significantly more satisfied. This finding confirms the importance of teacher autonomy identified by Wright. Barkdoll found a differential connection between stress and job satisfaction. For example, the most satisfied teachers reported low stress and high job satisfaction, while the least satisfied teachers reported high stress and low satisfaction.

There is no predominant reason that teachers cite for leaving teaching. Among the reasons are salary, limited opportunities for advancement, and too much to do in too little time. According to Ladwig, another common reason for leaving is lack of support from the principal. Principals may frequently (although not deliberately) reduce or eliminate a teacher's opportunities for intrinsic rewards.

Furthermore, factors such as low salary, low status, and excessive paperwork were found to be major sources of stress among teachers. However, the intention to leave teaching was more related to their coping resources. Marlow, Inmar, and Betancourt-Smith indicated that common reasons for leaving included problems with student discipline, lack of student motivation, and lack of respect from community, parents, administrators, and students.

Todd, Bame, Berry, Hacker, Hansen, Karsnitz, Radcliffe, Sanders, Ritz, & White addressed the problem of the teacher shortage in technology education. Several factors and recruitment strategies were suggested, but teacher satisfaction was not addressed. Information about "job-satisfiers" is essential if the technology education profession is to better understand the recruitment and preparation of new teachers. This is especially critical given the major changes that have occurred in technology education over the past 10-15 years.

Wright, using an in-depth interview technique based on Maslow's hierarchy of needs, found a significant positive relationship between technology teachers' perceived esteem and their job satisfaction. Esteem was derived from several sources, including pride in the profession, student respect, principal recognition, program respect, community support, and professional respect. Wright's analysis, focusing on the discrepancy between *desired* and (perceived) *actual* esteem, found that satisfaction was closely related to principal recognition, satisfaction with teaching assignment, years in current assignment, and job "autonomy." Salary was *not* a factor related to job satisfaction. The higher-order needs for esteem were most related to satisfaction. Carvelli also found that technology education teachers place high value on and flexibility in curriculum matters.

Research by Dugger, French, Peckham, & Starkweather report that the positive aspects of teaching technology include course content, staffing, and facilities, while weaknesses include funding, enrollment, and administrative support. The greatest problem was increased academic requirements. Other problems included lack of financial support, quality of students, and lack of administrative support. It is clear from the review that teacher satisfaction, although a complex phenomenon, affects student achievement, and vice versa. Teacher satisfaction findings tend to support Maslow's theory of needs-fulfilment. Specifically, esteem and self-actualisation on the job are factors having a significant impact on teacher satisfaction. Conversely, it would appear that "non-teaching" duties are a major source of dissatisfaction.

The two dominant "enjoyment" themes that emerged had to do with "excitement and stimulation of learning and working with new technologies," and "the enjoyment of working with kids and making a meaningful difference in their lives". The most frequently cited comments (20.5%) were classified as "enjoyment and stimulation of learning and using new technologies — continuous change." The second and third rated categories had to do with the enjoyment of working with students and the personal satisfaction of making meaningful differences in their lives.

The teachers' greatest satisfaction is also their greatest dissatisfaction. That is, they derive the most enjoyment from their students, while at the same time their students are one of their greater frustrations. One possible explanation is that experienced teachers had chosen to remain in teaching for the satisfaction that comes from helping students grow.

However, it is also possible that certain social and environmental factors over the past decade may have eroded the overall quality of the school climate, with corresponding declines in student behaviour and attitudes toward school. Thus, it may be that only a few students provide the disruption that so distracts from the teachers' overall enjoyment. "Lack of understanding and support of technology education by administrators/ counsellors" was the third most frequently cited, frustrating aspect of their jobs, followed by the "long hours required to deliver a quality program."

The top four frustrating aspects of teaching technology education are consistent with the literature and would likely be anticipated by most professionals in the field. What is surprising is that "low pay for teachers" was not in the top three factors (only 5% of the total responses). This finding is contrary to many national studies where poor compensation is typically among the top three factors cited. This finding is consistent with Wright's conclusion that certain intrinsic rewards (esteem and autonomy) offset (perceived) low pay, and that salary only becomes a serious issue when these intrinsic rewards are not present, or are greatly reduced.

The teachers listed "better funding for Technology Education programs" as the number one change needed by a factor of more than two-to-one over the second item, "public relations campaign to interpret what technology education is, its benefits, etc." This is consistent with the frustrations cited in the section above and with the findings of Dugger et al. that funding was the most serious challenge facing technology educators.

The actual magnitude of the significance of the funding factor may even be greater among the teachers included in this study. Indeed, there were seven other categories of responses that pertained to funding. These included "better compensation for teachers," "additional staff (more aides, etc.)," "additional corporate sponsorship for technology education," "assistance in seeking and obtaining funding for technology education program needs," "additional support to maintain laboratories and equipment," "support and recognition of additional extracurricular responsibilities," and "how schools are funded." Taken together, these categories comprise over one-third of all the comments related to what changes are needed.

The second major concern area dealt with educating the public and/or school officials about what technology education is, its benefits, etc., as well as differentiating it from instructional technology or educational technology. These comments ranged from "clarifying the purpose of technology education in the schools" to "public relations campaign to interpret what technology education is." The comments tended to focus on the lack of clarity and identification (and recognition of the) mission/purpose of technology education. The third broad area of concern was students, focusing on both student behaviour and academic ability.

The two primary reasons that these teachers like teaching technology is the excitement and stimulation of learning and working with new technologies, as well as the enjoyment of working with students. These teachers desire and receive a fair degree of autonomy in their daily jobs with regard to developing and implementing curriculum. The teachers in this study find the lack of funding and equipment, the decline in the personal characteristics of some students, and the lack of understanding and support of administrators and counsellors to be the most frustrating aspects of their jobs.

The overwhelming majority of the suggestions offered by the outstanding teachers may be summarised in two broad categories:

1) better funding and support for technology education, and

2) educating the public (and school personnel) about technology education.

If the technology education profession is to successfully attract and retain outstanding teachers, results of this study suggest that action must be undertaken to address these concerns. Technology education professionals or their associations cannot directly address issues such as better funding for schools/teachers or issues related to student discipline. However, the profession can appropriately address the major misconceptions regarding technology education and enlist the support of business and industry in doing so. This may help alleviate the two major concerns expressed by the teachers.

The following suggestions represent some practical and realistic steps for the technology education profession and its allied associations to take to address these concerns:

i) *In recruitment efforts, focus on the top three research findings: excitement of new technologies, enjoyment of working with kids, and independence and autonomy in daily routine.* The results of this study, and others, clearly indicate that the rewards of teaching technology are related to both the subject and the client! This information should be used by high school teachers and counsellors, university programs, and our professional associations as we attack the critical shortage of teachers in technology education. Individuals who are "people-oriented," that is, those who enjoy working with young people, and are excited about learning and using new technologies are the best candidates for becoming successful technology teachers. We need to be bold about suggesting technology teaching as a career option to people who seem to possess these qualities.

ii) The *Technology for All Americans Project* is an extremely valuable initiative to be used by the profession - not only for "standards" but also for educating school administrators, counsellors, boards of education, civic groups, and technology professionals.

iii) Linkages with colleges and universities (technical, design, and/or engineering). There is a great deal of activity occurring nationally with "2+2" articulation programs for trade and vocational programs. A similar model could be used for establishing linkages between technology education and teacher preparation programs.

iv) Local partnerships. Partnerships can be established with many different organisations/agencies including business and industry, other schools (such as elementary schools), and civic groups. These partnerships could create awareness and support for technology education.

v) Advisory committees. Advisory committees have many uses in addition to providing technical expertise. They may also be a means of involving/informing the public in/about the technology education program. Consider the role of the Technology Education Advisory Committee of the ITEA as an example.

vi) Local public exhibits and presentations. If the public and administrators are to better understand the purposes, scope, and sequence of technology education, then technology educators must assume the responsibility of "educating" them. This is a process that takes many years of conscientious effort, but there are numerous examples around the country where this has been done effectively. Exhibits may be set up at schools, shopping malls, and state fairs. Presentations can be made to the school board and local civic groups.

vii) *Massive national public relations blitz.* This is an effort that is sorely needed, but one that is probably beyond the resources of technology education professional associations. However, the associations could enlist a few large corporate sponsors. A one-page advertisement in *USA Today* or a 30-second spot on *CNN Evening News* could have awesome effects on heightening the visibility and understanding of technology education.

viii) *State, regional, and national grant writing workshops and support.* ITEA could provide a support structure for this initiative. Indeed, such an effort was initiated several years ago by Dr. Jane Liedtke with the support of the Technical Foundation of America. Such a program could be included at each state conference in addition to the national pre-conference workshops in order to assist teachers in obtaining additional resources.

Technology Education for Younger Learners

As the importance of a sound technological education for learners in their teenage years of schooling becomes accepted at a global level, there is increasing interest and belief in the need to start this education at an earlier age, possibly as soon as children begin formal schooling or even nursery school or kindergarten. Some teachers have warmly welcomed the challenge of introducing technology education to children at an early age. They have found that it has allowed them to develop new dimensions to work already underway. For others the idea has been received with more caution, for a variety of reasons.

Some are confused by what technology education would mean for young children. Others are concerned that limited resources would be stretched too thinly if the younger age group were included and that the primary curriculum is already overloaded. There are also those who believe that technology education is simply inappropriate with a younger age group.

Expanding the technology curriculum to primary schools raises a number of important issues. Any developments should be based on sound educational principles and thinking. Following are the key considerations:

i) the value of including technology in the curriculum for young children;

ii) critical dimensions to nurturing technological capability;

iii) appropriate models of teaching, learning and assessing;

vi) addressing the needs of the teacher; and

v) the importance of providing coherent, progressive and continuous technological experiences.

Human beings are born with the potential to develop as technologists. This is, in part, dependent on an amazing capacity of creating in our "mind's eye" new ideas and new configurations in order to make our world in the way we choose it to be. This capacity is something that sets us apart from other species in much the same way that our ability to develop and utilise complex linguistic systems does. Observing babies and toddlers as they busy about their world confirms the imaginative, inventive and determined way that, right from the start of life, we begin to utilise this creative capacity and to develop technological capability.

However, as with all aspects of development, creating the right conditions in which the potential can flourish is not necessarily straightforward. Technological capability is dependent on the ability to take action, to intervene in the made world, and to create new or improved products or systems. The children who are given more support to find out how things work, to make things work, and to create and to express themselves, the better chance there is for their technological capability to prosper. Children in the first years of life will encounter a wide variety of experiences.

For some there will be an abundance of opportunities to develop confidence and skill in those aspects that support technological capability. For others the opportunities will be limited. The range of experiences will be affected by a number of economic, social, cultural and philosophical influences and these in turn will impact on the way in which capability develops. There are, for example, indications of the effect that gender based expectations have on the early technological experiences of girls and boys and the consequences this has for children's development.

A main function of formal schooling is to take control over the experiences children have and to attempt to provide some equity in opportunities. If we accept that technology is an inherently important dimension of a child's curriculum, there is a logic to proposing that the earlier we, as educationalists, involve ourselves in this aspect of development, the better. Leaving this to chance, or at least until children enter secondary schooling seems a little haphazardous if not dangerous.

But introducing technology into the curriculum of young children is also important because of the propensity of this age group to engage in technological activity with an enthusiasm, curiosity and lack of inhibition that creates an optimum opportunity for development. Children's sheer excitement, wonder and enthusiasm for the world around them makes for an era of rapid development. In the preschool years, the child's lack of concern for external constraints allows for a free exploration of both their material and conceptual world. Curiosity as to how things work leads to a determination to make things work. Consequently, opportunities to develop problem solving skills are provided.

The more young children engage in technological activity, the more their confidence in their technological abilities may be established. Primary school teachers who have introduced technology into their curriculum often comment that technology activities are a valuable vehicle for all types of learning. This can include developing generic skills such as collaborative group working or problem solving, or more specific development of math or science concepts.

The technology activity often promotes a rich learning environment for a whole range of learning opportunities, thus providing an added value. Giving children a broad based experience of technology at a young age through which the foundations of technological capability can be consolidated and enhanced provides a basis from which to develop in a coherent and continuous way. But in planning technological experiences, teachers need to be aware of a range of factors that will have a bearing on development.

Ron Ritchie highlighted three critical features of learning situations that are significant for nurturing technological capability:

1) learning through practical experience;

2) an active learning process that allows children to construct their understanding of the world, and

3) learning within a social context.

Technology appears in several guises within curriculum documentation and taken, as a whole, three different formulations are clearly identifiable: courses that focus on developing awareness of technology (e.g., exploring it's impact on society), courses that focus on developing competence in technology (e.g., learning about electronics, learning how to shape a particular material) and courses that focus on developing capability in technology. These latter courses develop a pupil's holistic capability to put ideas into action to develop the made world. Put simply, these courses develop a child's ability to design what they make and to make what they design.

There is an important place for the development of awareness and competence (and indeed the three focuses are not necessarily mutually exclusive). But, it is the inclusive, holistic approach to developing capability that is the important focus with children in primary schools. Some might find this wrong faced. It could be argued that it is better to start with developing an awareness in young children and then building from this. But this would deny the important features highlighted by Ron Ritchie, and in particular the priority of learning through practical activity, so vital when considering the learning needs of young children.

In the second half of the 1980's in the United Kingdom a major research project was commissioned by the Assessment of Performance Unit (APU) of the Government Department for Education and Science that aimed to assess design & technological capability. The research focused on the nation's fifteen year olds and was conducted at Goldsmiths University of London under the direction of Richard Kimbell . One of the most significant outcomes from this project was an understanding of the iterative nature of the process that people engage in when designing and making and the importance of balancing the need to think about the task that has been undertaken (both reflectively and projectively) with the need to take action to turn ideas into working realities.

This work identified that both aspects are important (and their integration even more important) when considering the development of capability in fifteen year olds. Since then we have had the opportunity to consider this model of activity in relation to younger children and have found that it is equally applicable. This model has received corroboration from elsewhere and the importance of developing 'thought' skills and 'action' skills in primary age children is increasingly recognised as critical in technology.

Play has been seen by many educationalists as a critical factor in a child's development and this is particularly so of the development of technological capability. In particular "making and playing" can be seen as the early manifestation of capability, and the very act of being involved in play is crucial to the nurturing of this capability. This is largely due to the fact that play allows a child to enter into an imaginary world, through which they can gain first-hand experience in an unconstrained way. While not dealing directly with technological capability, Bruce sums up neatly the dimensions of play that provide the conditions through which technological capability can flourish, starting with the importance of firsthand experience.

Developing children's skills assists in the creation of positive attitudes such as self esteem and motivation and these attitudes in their turn help establish the conditions in which technological capability can thrive. However, such attitudes can be both built and destroyed through engagement in technological tasks and so it is important that children work in an environment that is at the same time supportive and challenging. They need opportunities to work on tasks that are within their capability, but that still have the potential to stretch them, where risk taking and failure are not seen as negative or handled destructively.

The need to develop just such a learning environment has been highlighted by teachers working on a primary technology initiative in the United States "Project Update". The teachers, who have by and large come afresh to technology activities have developed insights both by working through challenging tasks for themselves and by involving pupils in such activities. The resulting view is that the children should be involved in risk taking situations, where failure is seen as a positive learning experience and that this approach can prevent the children from placing "false ceilings on what they can learn and accomplish".

Technology is intrinsically a value laden phenomenon as developments are always driven by the needs, wants and aspirations of individuals or groups of people. Diverse needs mean that individuals will often perceive the impact of any technological solution differently - some may see a solution as good, while for others it is an unmitigating disaster (for example, automobiles are good for getting places, but bad for the environment).

Because this value laden position is a reality, it is important that children are encouraged to see the issues surrounding any technological decision, and to be involved in the decision making in a meaningful way. For this reason, primary teachers are increasingly involving children in technological tasks where the value positions are clear to the children and are presented in a way to which they can relate, such as the ways in which choice and use of materials impacts the environment.

Developing positive attitudes towards their peers and understanding the value of working with others is an important aim of technology education. Within this, the importance of children developing respect for each other, and in particular accepting the rights of all to engage in technological activities is vital in creating a nurturing learning environment.

This means that it is critical that technological activities take place in an atmosphere where stereotypes are countered and differentiation strategies are utilised to allow all children to realise their potential. This is particularly so in primary schools as value positions can be adopted at a very young age, and if not challenged by real and positive examples can become intransigent.

Technology activities are particularly rich in potential for allowing all children to succeed, thus providing living proof to challenge negative assumptions. However, in order to support the development of all children, particular consideration needs to be given to the ways in which young children learn and consequently the range of experiences that teachers need to structure for them.

In order to operate effectively, children must develop a range of contributory skills - procedural, manipulative and communicative. This must occur alongside conceptual understandings, both of how to make things work and how to meet people's needs and wants. Few people would disagree with this standpoint, but the way in which such contributory skills are best developed often is the cause for disagreement.

The ways in which primary education has developed in different parts of the globe will relate very much to the traditions and ethos of the culture in which it has developed. In the United Kingdom, while there are differences between one school and the next, the overarching model of learning in primary schools is one which is seen as "child centered" and in which children are viewed as active learners.

This means that, for many young children in the UK, their school (and hence their technology) experience will be managed in a classroom environment which lacks the formality of the secondary school, where much work will be handled in an integrated way, initiated by topics or themes.

Moreover, children will be familiar with working both collaboratively and individually. Similar models will be found elsewhere in the world, but some cultures will have a different tradition.

It is important to identify these differences here, in order to put what follows in context, as many of the examples used are drawn either from the UK or from school systems that have elements in common with this approach. It will therefore be important that readers evaluate each model, strategy and example that is given in terms of the value it holds for developments within their own school setting.

Any debate about approaches to teaching and learning technology in education must consider the often conflicting claims for priority in addressing educational or vocational needs. For very young children, the focus and priority must be on their educational development.

Indeed it's important that educators protect their rights to remain children. The issues of the development of their technological capability should not be clouded by introducing such issues as the economic well being of a nation or how a work force is going to be trained for the next generation.

This is not to say that we shouldn't be concerned for the future of the children and do our best to ensure that they develop their potential to lead happy and satisfying lives as adults. It is more to suggest that the specifics of the technological experience of six year olds should not be planned by looking at the skills required for them to pass examinations at the end of compulsory schooling, or those that will allow them to become the mechanical engineers, architects or food technologists of the future.However it's important to consider two further dimensions within this. First there is increasing acceptance that general technological competencies are more appropriate for young children in a rapidly changing technological society than are specific skills.

By developing a more generic potential from a young age, this next generation may be more comfortable, confident, and secure in their own capability. As a result, they may be in a better position to utilise it flexibly across a wide range of settings. Where these skills are developed through an integrative, holistic approach, there may be greater propensity for them to be utilised in a broad range of settings, hence furthering the potential of technology education. It is also important that knowledge and skill are not seen only in terms of vocational development. The introduction and development of knowledge and skill on "need-to-know" basis can serve to enhance the developing capability as young children resolve tasks in a satisfying rather than frustrating way. Readiness for learning is an important concept - trying to introduce a new skill or concept to a learner too early can at best be wasteful of time and at worst damaging to their confidence if they perceive themselves as a failure.

The concept of teaching knowledge and skills in technology on a need-to-know basis, introducing new material to children at the point they need it to further pursue their designing and making, pays attention to the notion of readiness, but goes further to highlight the importance of teaching something new in context.

In recent classroom research conducted at Goldsmiths (the UTA Project1) this approach was very effective. In one instance, a 5 year old was designing and making a house for a toy spider. He had made a slide for the spider to play on, but was concerned that the spider couldn't get to the top of the slide. He thought a ladder would be the answer, but needed to know how to make one. The teacher intervened at this point, first to support him to visualise and then draw a ladder, and then to introduce new skills of measuring, marking and cutting wooden dowel and using a low melt glue gun to join the ladder together.

The timing was just right, and having developed and consolidated his new skills, the child went on to use them in further work. An older child, age 10, was making a model fairground carousel. She had an idea that it was possible to power the carousel using weights and pulleys, but had no understanding of how this could be done. The teacher stepped in and worked with the child to introduce new understandings about pulleys and then supported the child to utilise this new knowledge to make her roundabout work. In a third incident a whole group was working on making model houses and supermarkets for an exhibition.

At the point at which they needed to make stable models of their structures, the teacher demonstrated a range of ways of doing this. Introducing new knowledge when the need is triggered by the project allows a teacher to identify opportunities for progression and critical windows for supporting this. We concluded that it is vital that pupils are engaged in designing and making that is just within or just beyond their reach. This challenges them constantly to extend into new understandings in order to achieve success.

A complementary approach, particularly in relation to developing new conceptual understandings, is the use of problem solving. As mentioned earlier, finding out by solving problems is a strategy used by very young children long before they engage in formal schooling. The UTA Project was particularly conscious of the effective use of this approach with older primary children (8-11 year olds). We the researchers witnessed a range of new understandings being developed in this way: a child working out how to make a slipper that would fit his foot by experimenting with scissors, paper and pins to make a working model; a pair of children working out how to make a tiller for a galleon that could genuinely be used to steer it; a child working out how to make a Venetian blind for a model house she was making; and so forth.

In all cases, the solving of the problem became a motivational hook and the sense of challenge and achievement was tangible. Problem solving inevitably involves children in risk taking situations and it is important that it is conducted in a supportive atmosphere. It is equally important that the teacher is on hand to either provide prompts if a child meets a challenge that is too demanding to be achieved independently, or to provide answers that counter any misconceptions a child might develop.

Again linked closely to the previous approach is a belief in learning through hands on exploration in the context of problem solving research. In their collection of activities from across Europe, Benson & Raat include a valuable example of young children researching material properties through hands on exploration. Six and seven year old children were provided with a collection of different types of wire and gauze and simple tools that could be used to cut and bend them. They were introduced to an activity aimed at finding out as much as possible. They did this first by observing and then by manipulating about the way the wires could be bent, cut and twisted. Initially they explored possibilities in a free way and then explored ways of using their experience to identify technical and decorative uses. This kind of activity builds on the approach very young children adopt to find out about their world. While it is in many ways quite structured, its antecedents can be seen in the free flow play of the toddler, as can it's value in developing both understanding and mastery.

The UTA Project, found that hands on exploration was a useful way for children to model design ideas. Working directly with materials appeared to free children to think in 3 dimensions, to work kinesthetically with materials and create their designs by trial and error. But, they did this with a growing understanding of the working properties of the material. This was particularly evident with one ten year old child who used this approach to build a complete model staircase, including a landing that turned the staircase through 90 degrees.

A great deal of concern has been expressed in the UK that the development of technology in the curriculum of young children should not be dominated by paradigms developed in secondary schools, or seen as a mere watering down of work done with older pupils. These concerns have related as much to the approach to work as to the content of lessons. Some of these concerns have been confirmed by situations where a primary teacher has, for want of any other example, employed secondary school approaches, only to find them ill suited to supporting the needs of the children.

An illustration of this has been seen in approaches to getting children to generate ideas where the perceived approach has been to ask the children to design what they want to make, in advance, by drawing on paper. This has led to frustration for teachers because they have been uneasy with the relationship between what the children drew, what they eventually went on to make (often bearing little resemblance to the initial drawing) and a growing sense that the act of making the drawing was not supporting the child's process or development.

It has also led at times to frustration on the part of the children. The act of trying to express a 3D artifact through 2D on paper (an act that Angela Anning so aptly points out "would tax many adults") provides confusion and complexity rather than clarity - a clarity that perhaps would have been more attainable by modeling the idea directly in 3 dimensions using construction kits, modeling clay, paper or cardboard.

This concern, particularly in relation to the procedures children use in technology tasks has prompted recent research in the UK focusing specifically on the early years. Cy Roden's work with 5 year olds has raised issues about whether the strategies commonly used by young children are replaced by others as they get older, and suggests that there may be an optimal time for the development of any strategy. This raises the need for further consideration being given to indiscriminately introducing a strategy to one age group that is utilised with older learners. Findings of the UTA Project clearly indicate that children of the same age utilise different working styles, and given the freedom to do so, adopt procedures that best suit their own style. Perhaps the key message here is that, whatever their age, a range of different and appropriate strategies should be accepted and encouraged. What is most important is that children express and develop ideas. The ways in which they do this should be seen as a means to an end and not an end in themselves.

Teaching within meaningful contexts is important in bringing relevance to an activity and to help children take ownership of tasks they undertake. Within technology education the context serves a further purpose. The context becomes a vehicle to bring the design issues into the open. Children designing homes for toy spiders have to think about a range of criteria that relate to creating successful homes keeping dry and warm, creating a stimulating environment and so on. By addressing such considerations, the task the children are engaged in becomes richer and the children's decision making more thoughtful. One very important strategy that helps a child engage with a context is to use fantasy or role play. This was the case with a group of six year old children whose teacher had taken the topic of explorers for the focus of their work.

Through role play and imagination, the class had gone on a sea voyage, been chased by pirates, shipwrecked and subsequently washed up on a deserted island. The children enacted the experience of spending their first night on the island - with nowhere to sleep, nothing to keep them warm and dry, and nothing to protect themselves from wild animals and the pirates. As a result, the children identified the need to build shelters and set about designing and making model shelters that would provide warmth and protection, that would allow rain to run off, that were camouflaged from the pirates, and that had secure entrances, some protected by booby traps, should the pirates track them down.

Each decision that was made was governed by the fantasy situation but was made in a critical and thoughtful way. In order to realise their designs, children needed to develop new skills and understandings such as how to make a pointed roof, how to make a house on stilts that didn't wobble, and how to make a fence that contained a hinged gate. The level of learning was made possible by the willingness of the children to engage in the fantasy world.

The model of technology being promoted here is one in which children are thinkers as well as doers. Consequently the teaching and learning approach needs to be structured to develop children's ability to reflect on their work. Young children develop many skills initially at a tacit level. They may, for example, have developed skills in cutting cardboard shapes accurately without being conscious of how they do it. As educationalists, it is important that we help children turn their tacit understandings into explicit ones - to be 'metacognitive' about their experience. Providing opportunities for reflection and resourcing these with appropriate prompts is critical in achieving this. There are good examples of teachers facilitating this by encouraging children to use devices such as logs and process diaries.

Putting children in a position where they take responsibility for their actions was seen as one way of achieving this in Project Update. The author gives the example of children asking the teacher when their project would be finished. The question was turned back on the children - when did they think it would be over? The children discussed this and then replied, "It will be over when it does what we said it would do." The Project reporters point out that this statement showed that the children "had to re-examine their thinking to determine what constituted an adequate purpose," a process which required them to bring their thinking out into the open, thus making it explicit and available for reflecting upon.

Supporting the children to develop reflective skills will also facilitate the way in which they can evaluate both the outcomes of their task and the progress they have made. This self assessment has often been a feature of the logs and process diary approach and can contribute to the overall assessment by the teacher. By involving the child in the process, they are empowered to take control over their own learning. This approach has been piloted across the primary age range, starting with 5 year olds.

If such assessment relates directly to project work, then the assessment process can be integrated into the learning process. Children can assess themselves and be assessed by their teacher while working on task thereby allowing for "authentic assessment." However, it is important to distinguish between monitoring a child's experience (in order that the teacher can keep track of the experience and use this to help plan a broad and balanced curriculum) and assessing the capability they display (in order to keep track of the child's progress and, within this, strengths to be built on and weaknesses to be addressed).

It is also important to consider what is the most appropriate model of assessment to be utilised. As has been discussed earlier, technological capability is an integrative capability that draws on and draws together a person's knowledge, skill and understandings. Because of it's integrative nature, the capability is best developed in an holistic way, and hence assessed in a holistic way.

This approach allows teachers to build an overall picture of a child's capability, within which they can look to diagnose specific strengths and weaknesses. Once identified, action for development can be taken within the context of the child's overall capability, identifying strategies (that can perhaps be shared with the child) to develop specific areas, such as a child's ability to plan, to reflect, to make and so on.

Developing technological capability requires teachers to structure activities and inputs in such a way that what children learn, in terms of procedures, concepts and skills, is "taught not caught". Moreover, the children should be active participants in this process. This is not to marginalise experiential learning or to discount the potential of serendipity, but rather to identify the importance of teachers taking an active role in determining both the what and the how of the learning. This means that teachers need to have the personal knowledge, skill and confidence to resource this, which, because of a lack of training provision, is not often possible. It is therefore important to now turn to those issues that relate to meeting the needs of the teachers involved in the enterprise.

Earlier the importance of the 'readiness' of children to learn was emphasised. This concept is equally important when considering how teachers can be supported to engage successfully in technology education.

Very few primary teachers have received formal training in the teaching of technology education. Even those countries that have decided to introduce compulsory technology education into their primary curriculum, and who have set up training programs to facilitate this, have a back log of unprepared technology educators teaching in primary schools. The task of providing professional development for them all is massive. Our experience in the UK (where by some standards there has been a considerable input of resources, although nowhere near enough to meet teachers' needs), suggests key areas to be addressed in helping teachers move forward include:

— developing teacher's understanding of what technology education is;

— helping them see how the work they currently do, and the experience they already have, can be adapted to allow technology activities to grow from the work already undertaken with the children;

— developing their confidence in their ability to build on and utilise their previous experience;

— identifying a broad but manageable range of activities for teachers to start from, and providing them with personal, hands on experience with the activities before they embark on them with children;

— providing opportunities (through dialogue and printed materials) for teachers to share good ideas and good practice and build a repertoire of successful activities.

Pilot projects that have been structured to address the above areas have provided good models to build on and have illustrated both issues to be dealt with and strategies that contribute to success. Taking each of the key areas above and illustrating them from some of the work that has taken place in recent years will perhaps help clarify some ways forward.

From 1990-1992, we at Goldsmiths developed a set of National optional assessment tasks to help primary teachers assess technology capability. This project was linked to the introduction of the National Curriculum in Technology and the tasks were designed not only to help teachers make assessments, but also to help them structure and manage technology activities (sometimes for the first time). Teachers were very confused about technology - was it computers, applied science, or craftwork? We wanted them to understand the simple message that technology was about designing and making products that would meet peoples needs and desires and that the children needed to 'design what they made and make what they designed'.

The Learning in Technology Education project, carried out in New Zealand from 1992-1994, involved both primary and secondary teachers for this same purpose. Introducing technology education to the primary teachers illustrated several parallels with the researchers' experience in the UK. At the start of the venture the primary teachers expressed similar confusions about the nature of technology education. But again, following a process of discussing technology education, exploring exemplar activities and then planning, implementing and evaluating their own activities, it became evident that the teachers' understanding (and with it their confidence) had grown.

In both of these examples, certain aspects are worth highlighting: the teachers were involved in first hand activity; they had opportunities to discuss what they were doing with others going through the same experience; and they were actively encouraged to evaluate their experience. Just as is so valuable with children, the teachers were provided with the opportunity for action and reflection to be both 'thinkers' and 'doers'.

Once primary teachers become involved in a technology activity, they realise how much they can draw both on their general teaching skills and also on work from other areas such as science, mathematics, and art. Working from strengths is important, but within this it is necessary to help teachers see how previous work might need a shift in emphasis to develop as a technology project. This was the case with a teacher who had taken a topic of "Down our street" with a Year 2 class. This topic initiated science work as children explored the materials the street and the buildings were made from, history work as they investigated the history of street lighting, and art work as they drew the local buildings and made a street scene frieze.

However, the teacher was having trouble locating a starting point for the technology work. Following discussions during which we explored the importance of the concept of need and purpose in technology, she introduced to the class an idea that they should think of ways of "improving our street." The addition of this one word, and the shift in emphasis it indicated had an amasing effect on the children's imaginations and within no time they had changed their classroom into a planning office, redesigned the signs and blinds over local shops, explored ways of designing pavements by laying paving slabs in interesting patterns, and building a model to show how the street could be turned into a pedestrian precinct.

In the Goldsmiths project, in a questionnaire aimed at identifying the primary teachers' state of readiness to teach technology, there was a common pattern to the teachers' feelings about their own strengths and weaknesses. Often seen as an area promoting confidence was the teacher's ability to introduce and discuss work with children, whereas a common lack of confidence related to lack of skills to support children's making. This latter concern is a very real one and is the reason behind much primary technology in-service work being focused in this area.

An approach that breeds both confidence and skill in supporting children's making, is one which provides teachers with opportunities for hands-on practical work themselves. This is common in in-service courses in England and was a feature of the early work done with teachers involved in *Project Update* in the USA. The value of such activity is that the teachers not only develop the specific skills required, but the activity also provides a reference point for planning classroom activities how long will the activity take, what resources are needed, what will the children need to be taught, will it be best for them to work as individuals or in groups? Teachers are able to see how best to manage the activity.

An outcome of each of the three projects mentioned here was a collection of classroom activities to be shared. The optional assessment tasks were trialed and evaluated (though not initiated) by the teachers, and modified accordingly before being made available to all teachers in England and Wales.

The Learning in Technology Education project produced examples initially of activities drawn up by the research team, but once the teachers had planned and trialed their own, these were added into the bank. *Project Update* has been set up with a clear aim of supporting the teachers involved to become curriculum writers, as their planned, trialed and evaluated activities are edited into a collection of classroom materials supporting not just technology, but also science and mathematics.

In any area that is as new to the primary curriculum as technology is, sharing good ideas and good practice is imperative. Developing a repertoire of good practice not only enables new teachers to be "fast forwarded" into the venture, it also builds a solid foundation that gives confidence within the profession.

Women and Technology Education

Every woman has been a technological being, using and often inventing tools, materials, and processes in order to adapt and modify her world. Their contributions have been either focused on the traditional homemaking roles of females, or they have been diminished in the records of industrial and economic spheres. In addition to diminishing the role of women in technology and engineering, many technical occupations, including science, have a low representation of women. Are there differences between women and men which might influence their choice of study and which need to be addressed? Can technology educators begin to address the lack of participation of women and girls in technology education without understanding the potential for differences between men and women with regard to technology and to education?

There is a rainbow of feminist theories which suit the ideological bent of women who espouse them. In an overview of feminism, Donovan described feminists as liberal; cultural; related to other theories such as Freudianism, Marxism, existentialism, etc.; radical; promoting a new feminist moral vision; and ecofeminists. Essentially, *liberal-feminists* have called attention to the inequality in society and have proposed remedies to that inequality. *Cultural feminists* have created a rationale for the differences in male and female cultures. *Feminists influenced by other philosophies* such as existentialism and postmodernism have interacted with those philosophies by both applying them to feminist ideas and principles and influencing the root philosophy with feminist ideas and principles.

Radical feminists blame patriarchy as the cause of all societal problems and seek to supplant it with women's modes of thinking and acting. *Ecofeminists* incorporate several of the previously mentioned views into a theory of feminist values for the good of the environment. *Feminists of the new moral vision* integrate cultural feminism sans radical feminism in order to address inequity to create, for women and men, not just inclusion in a male dominated society, but a means of promoting the value of women's ways of thinking and acting. It is this category of feminist thought which underpins the discussion here.

Clearly, the dominant culture in Western society is the male culture, not by size but by influence. Evidence of this exists in the roles which women take on in relation to men, the valuing of traditional female roles in economic theory which historically has not factored in the contributions of women in the home, the traditional use of language to prefer male pronouns to indicate all humans, and the inability of politicians and citizens to successfully support an equal rights for women amendment to the Constitution. These and many other indications of the subjugation of the female in a hierarchy of value are explicitly evident in Greek philosophy, the bedrock of Western thought. Essentially, women are relegated to second class status or invisibility in Western culture.

There are some who doubt the power of language and "ancient" philosophy, but Greek philosophical concepts persist in our culture through our use of language. About using the generic term "Man," Minnich provides a powerful illustration by using the rules of syllogistic logic that have been handed down from Greek philosophers.

Consider the famous syllogism: 'Man is mortal. Socrates is a man. Therefore, Socrates is mortal.' Try it with a woman: 'Man is mortal. Alice is' what? A man? No one says that, not even philosophers. 'Man,' the supposedly generic term, does not allow us to say, 'Alice is a woman.' Then what are we to deduce? 'Therefore, Alice is' what? ...Reason flounders; the center holds, with Man in it, but it is an exclusive, not universal or neutral, center. Alice disappears through the looking glass.

The use of language is powerful in shaping our thoughts, but Greek philosophy has shaped more than our thoughts through the use of language. It has shaped our actions. Modern science is based in the rationalism and logical positivism inherited from our heritage of Greek philosophy. The rationale and argument which reinforced the duality of logic as science and emotion as nature and assigned gender characteristics to these concepts is found in Greek philosophy, especially the philosophy of Plato. According to a host of philosophers, both male and female, modern science is founded upon Plato's philosophy summarised this thinking. Modern science can thus be said to be following Plato's script, but without heeding his cautionary advice. In this script it appears inevitable that intercourse with physical nature evokes the domination and aggression appropriate to women and slaves.

Western science and technology have evolved based upon the concept of predicting and controlling nature, and nature has been assigned the female gender by Western philosophers.

Adding to the philosophy which has enabled the growth of Western science and technology was Bacon who furthered the arguments for power and domination of nature. Bacon helped to further separate the world into a duality, the mind as knower (masculine) and nature (feminine) as the knowable, a division into man as knower and subject and woman as knowable and object, placing man the subject and knower in control of women the object and knowable. Through science and art (that is, technology, or mechanical art), man can find the power to transform not so much the world as his relation to the world. The goal of science was, for Bacon, 'the restitution and reinvesting of man to the sovereignty and power ...which he had in his first state of creation'.

In Western philosophy, through the language and metaphor, as well as through the history of practice, science and technology have become intertwined and linked to masculinity. Linked to science through the concept of applied science, technology assumes the masculine connotations given to science as an activity of power and conquest over nature.

As an activity in itself, technology is an attempt to control nature, becoming another example of where gender assignment is made to the subject as control. Reinforcement of gender characteristics is carried out in duality of technology and nature and the metaphor of technology as masculine dominating nature as feminine.

Masculine here connotes, as it so often does, autonomy, separation, and distance. It connotes radical rejection of any commingling of subject and object, which are, it now appears, quite consistently identified as male and female.

While Bacon provided stepping stones of ideas for the growth of Western philosophy of science, Descartes has been given the credit for reifying the masculinisation of Western scientific and technological thought. Philosophers tend to agree that Descartes provided the arguments and rationale for attributing masculinity to rational and logical thought in science and technology.

The notion that the project of modern science crystallises 'masculinist' modes of thinking has been a prominent theme in some recent writing: '[What] we encounter in Cartesian rationalism,' says Karl Stern, 'is the pure masculinisation of thought.' The scientific model of knowing, says Sandra Harding, represents a 'super-masculinisation of rational knowledge.' 'The specific consciousness we call scientific, Western and modern,' claims James Hillman, 'is the long sharpened tool of the masculine mind that has discarded parts of its own substance, calling it 'Eve,' 'female' and 'inferior.''

Descartes provided for the separation of subject and object in philosophy and in science and technology, separating thought and logic from nature. Separation and individuation are strong themes in Descartes work with separation and detachment as essential characteristics for the scientific and technological mind.

According to Descartes, achieving this separation depends upon a "rebirth," one which sheds the mystical and illogical images of nature so predominant during the Middle Ages. This change to autonomous logic is needed in order to reconstruct knowledge, especially scientific and technological knowledge, and the mysticism of nature is cast as feminine in order to separate logical thought from nature.

Situating this masculine birth—or more precisely, *rebirth*—within the context of the cultural separation anxieties described earlier, it appears not only as an intellectual orientation but as a mode of denial as well, a reaction formation to the loss of 'being-one-with-the-world' brought about by the disintegration of the organic, centered cosmos of the Middle Ages and Renaissance. The Cartesian reconstruction of the world is a defiant gesture of independence from the female cosmos—a gesture that is at the same time compensation for a profound loss.

Philosophers of all schools have given credit to Bacon and Descartes for creating the ideological framework for the growth of Western science. Much of the way in which science and technology are conducted today is a result of these fundamental ideas which shaped the procedures of science. Yet, as with any human endeavour, the influence of Bacon and Descartes has not been permanent, as the conduct of science continues to evolve. Many philosophers, especially those of the Frankfurt school have and are contributing to the reunification of the subject and the object in order to both develop new ways of conducting science and technology and to explain the reality of what is happening as science is conducted and technology is created. A continual revolution of scientific thinking as described by Kuhn is taking place. To this revolution, feminists have much to contribute to the dispelling of the Cartesian duality in philosophy and science, and eventually, in daily life. Feminist theories can influence how educators conduct education in general and how technology educators specifically conduct their classes in order to be inclusive.

The current discussion of women's ways of knowing in feminist literature represents a severe critique of liberal feminism. Essentially, the position of a number of current feminists is that women, constituted as the other, do function in different ways than men and that their ways of knowing have much to offer in the reconstruction of theory. Using the discussion of cultural differences, contemporary feminists are trying to create an alternate theory and scientific methodology based upon the differences of women. The purpose of this is not to destroy science, but to continue the evolution of science.

Two thrusts are evident in women's literature about science: discussing the masculine bias as outlined above and arguing for a different, feminist influence in science. The framework of ideas for a more inclusive form of science include:

One in which no rigid boundary separates the subject of knowledge (the knower) and the natural object of that knowledge; where the subject/object split is not used to legitimise the domination of nature. Where nature itself is conceptualised as active rather than passive, a dynamic and complex totality requiring human cooperation and understanding rather than a dead mechanism, requiring only manipulation and control...the scientist is not seen as an impersonal authority standing outside and above nature and human concerns, but simply a person whose thoughts and feelings, logical capacities, and intuitions are all relevant and involved in the process of discovery.

This form of science is not considered to be the exclusive domain of women, but of both sexes. The purpose of such science is to enable scientists to continue to progress, revising faulty interpretations and theories which rested on the assumption of masculine power and domination.

Harding characterises such a science as having new empirical and theoretical resources of women's experiences, new purposes for social science as women, and new subject matter for inquiry by locating the researcher in the same critical plane as the overt subject matter. Essentially, this kind of science is being developed in many areas. One of the most famous illustrations of this change in the view of science has been detailed by Fox Keller in her biography of Barbara McClintock. As a Nobel Laureate for her pioneering work in the plant genetics, McClintock's approach to her study involved a more contextual research process by observing the growing of corn in fields, the natural environment; holding back on hypotheses and imposition of answers; and valuing the exceptions.

Another area of research which has benefited from feminist conceptions of theory and paying attention to women's ways of knowing has been the work of primatologists as outlined by Reed, Haraway, and Hrdy and as given notoriety by the work of Dian Fossey with mountain gorillas. Fossey and other women have been able to reinterpret, explain, and develop more accurate primate theory by rejecting masculine theories of domination and control in primate societies and by observing, closely, the actual interactions and social behaviours of primates.

While women's participation has been changing the way in which science is conceptualised and conducted as illustrated by the previous examples, a specific area of behavioural science, psychology, is also being questioned and revised with a concern for eliminating the inherent gender bias in Western science. This revision is directly related to differences in women's ways of thinking and knowing.

If women do think and learn differently than men, then we need to address those differences in education, especially in the context of technology education where there is a severe lack of women. It could be that technology educators have not examined the philosophy and psychology of women's thinking in order to learn how to be more inclusive of women in both technology education and creating technology.

By the lack of numbers, it appears as though women are avoiding the study of technology education. Young girls view it as a male subject. Some of this effect is due to a history of exclusion and stereotyping with respect to course of study, yet we do not seem to be changing the traditional separation of girls into home economics and boys into technology education.

For those few technology educators who are concerned about this problem, the discussion has centered on the "chilly" classroom effect known to exist in subjects not traditionally studied by many women and the "add women and stir" method of resolving the problem. Unfortunately, "add women and stir" has not been known to be a successful cure in other subjects. It appears as though the problem is much deeper than socialising girls and women into the existing hierarchy.

Perhaps, we need to rethink the hierarchy and technology education content and practice. The descriptions of women's ways of knowing have multiple meanings for technology educators. Some of the ideas help to cast doubt on and dispel the dominance of masculine thinking in science and technology. The arguments could lead to reconceptualising science and technology as we now know it, incorporating a larger concern for context and environment and a diminishing concern for control and domination. As the school subject representing the study of technology, technology education has been a male controlled subject matter defined by males.

Technology educators could revise their view of the role and purpose of technology, especially as they approach the study of technology in the classroom. Another way that this information could influence technology educators is the way in which they construct activities for children in classrooms. If women are to be attracted to a study of technology, both the value and purpose of technology and the way in which it is taught must be changed. Several women in other educational fields have tried to provide direction in order to help teachers to implement feminist ideals in their pedagogy.

Certainly, these ideas are not new and they are advocated by male educators seeking to improve the practice of education in general. The ideas focus on creating a critical pedagogy. Goals, based upon feminist theory include restructuring the subject matter, revising language, creating a humane classroom, and integrating cognitive and affective learning. These goals relate to the issues of revising the subject matter and recognising women's ways of thinking and acting mentioned above, and, they go far beyond a simplistic add women and stir.

Feminists as well as many men are suggesting alternatives to the traditional masculine models of power and domination for the reconstruction of technology. In a series of lectures, Franklin described the current state of technology as a system and as practice linked to culture. She defined technology as prescriptive and depending upon compliance, leading to isolation, control, and planning to maximise efficiency. These thoughts are echoed by a number of women who have studied the interaction of women and technology. Franklin (1990) noted the feminist critique of technology and its intent to revise, not destroy science and technology. As an engineer, herself, she does not seek to destroy technology as we know it, but to redefine technology.

While noting that the technologies, advocates for change, and means to change exist, Franklin called for a conserver society in which technological decisions are made with humility by taking into account nature and people first. In order to do this she recommends that we listen to ecofeminists and cultural feminists and learn to communicate with each other in order to examine the costs and benefits of our technological choices to society. The purpose of this would be to develop technologies which are appropriate in scale and application. Finally, she suggests that, "We must protest until there is *change* in the structures and practices of the real world of technology, for only then can we hope to survive as a global community".

Feminist theorists have created an interpretation of technology as a largely masculine enterprise, relying upon domination and control of the environment. Ecofeminists have critiqued patriarchy as being largely responsible for technological abuses of nature and suggest alternatives driven by feminist ideals for addressing environmental concerns. Technology educators interested in studying the environment and discussing the nature of technology in our society can incorporate the feminist critique, as well as critiques based upon race and class, of technology into the curriculum of technology education.

Using feminist, racial, and class theory and critique would give voice to the concerns of not only women, but also other under represented groups in the content of what is taught as technology education. Comparing all of these critiques to the ongoing critique and discussion of technology would allow students to contrast thinking about technology in order to look for similarities and differences. More important, the critical discussion of technology and the way in which we, as a society, choose to implement technology, especially as a society in which gender, race, and class structures create inequities in power, would give students insight into how to subvert prescriptive technologies in favour of developing redemptive technologies.

Addressing the critiques of technology would benefit all students by helping them to understand that technology is a debatable practice with both positive and negative consequences for the environment and different groups of people. Teaching about the critiques of technology and their corresponding philosophical rationales would add depth and rigor to the study of technology.

In addition to the concerns presented above with respect to revising language, technology educators need to observe and think about how women use technology. Women as technology users often co-opt the technology as originally designed and utilise it to further their values, particularly their need to communicate.

From the telephone to e-mail, as women have encountered communication technologies they have been quick to utilise them to maintain contact with other people, displaying characteristic women's ways of knowing such as having a need for context and explanation. Women as a group have also approached the use of computers, especially computer games, with some differences.

Not as many girls as boys are as entertained by the "shoot 'em up" games, yet they do engage in the "building up" games and use the creative tool software. In recent research about gender differences with respect to technology, Welty found that women identified communication and medical technologies more frequently than men. Technology educators need to understand that women's values will enter into their valuing and use of technology and that women will find ways of using the technology for their own priorities, just as any one should.

Using design briefs as cooperative activities is a good way to initiate change based in feminist theories. When technology teachers create activities such as design briefs for students, some knowledge and empathy with women's ways of knowing and acting could help them to create design briefs that might be of interest to girls and women. Not everyone wants to design a machine tool.

Some women do, yes, but others may be more interested in designing a device to aid a handicap, a decorative item, toy, or other object that would require the same knowledge and skills as designing and making a machine tool. What seems to be valid and appealing to teachers may not always be appealing and valid to students, both females and males.

The ideal would be to identify the concept, processes, and skills, which need to be taught and cast them into a design brief which would allow each student to interpret the solution as she or he sees fit.

A good example of this kind of activity is discussed in research on problem solving by McCormick, Murphy, Henessey, and Davidson where in a technology class students were to devise moisture sensors and to provide an application for them. One of the students in the class created a fake stocking to hang on a clothesline in order to sound an alarm when it rained. This application is unique to the student and not something that would be suggested by most technology teachers.

Based upon the discussion of the inherent masculine values in the creation and conduct of science and technology as presented by several feminist theorists, it is difficult to deny that values are not a part of the curriculum. It is from the feminist discussion that we can see that the denial of values, the separation of subject and object, leads us to reproducing default values of masculinity which influences science, technology, and the curriculum.

In any human endeavour, values are inescapable. Teachers need to begin to address and to incorporate values in their curriculum through study of various value positions, discussion and critique of values, and value laden activities in order to avoid hegemony, the unconscious reproduction of values.

Technology education is often approached as a series of processes and techniques that are taught in isolation of the affective values which accompanies all human activity. There are many technology educators who are trying to revise the curriculum of the field in order to include a broader knowledge base and the values associated with technology, particularly the technological systems. More specifically, a number of technology educators are recommending the study of technology education from a social reconstruction perspective.

Social reconstruction curriculum confronts the value question by making the improvement of society, a value-laden activity, a fundamental principle of curriculum selection and organisation. Technology educators need to continue to blend the cognitive and affective aspects of technology education in order to improve technology education for all children. Adopting a social reconstruction curriculum design is one way to do this. In addition to addressing the values inherent in technology to begin creating a participative, inquiry driven classroom, Miller suggests:

Situated narratives of educational experience and inquiry, expressed in multiple versions and forms, offer ways into examinations of such complex intersections and constructions of both identities and curriculum. Current versions of such studies point to work in autobiography, including dialogue journals, life histories of students and teachers, descriptions and analyses of situated pedagogies and curricular practices, 'teacher and student lore,' and 'teachers' personal practical knowledge.' Technology teachers need to experiment with unique ways of permitting students to express their values with respect to technology in non-threatening ways through a combination of learning activities.

Bibliography

Brooksfield, S.D., *The Skillful Teacher: On Technique, Trust, and Responsiveness in the Classroom,* San Francisco, CA: Jossey-Bass, 1990.

Burow-Flake, E., Kocher, D., Reiser, A., *Changing Students, Changing Classroom Landscapes: Meeting the Challenge in the Small Liberal Arts Institution,* in L. Lloyd (ed.), *Teaching with Technology, Rethinking Tradition,* Medford, NJ: Information Today, Inc., 2000.

Cohen, J. A., Castner, M. H., *Technology and Classroom Design: A Faculty Perspective,* in L. Lloyd (ed.), *Teaching with Technology, Rethinking Tradition,* Medford, NJ: Information Today, Inc., 2000.

Duhaney, D., Technology and the Educational Process: Transforming Classroom Activities, *International Journal of Instructional Media,* 27(1), pp.67-72, 2000.

Hezel Associates, *Educational Telecommunications, State By State Analysis,* Syracuse, NY, 1994.

Kelch, P. E., Karr-Kidwell, P. J., *How Computer Technology Expands Educational Options: A Rationale, Recommendations and a Pamphlet for Administrators,* ERIC Document Reproduction Service, no. 439 668, 2000.

Regan, K., and Tuchman, S., "The Importance of Authority and Peer Relations on the Educational Process of Onsite and Online Communications", *Computers and Education,* 1993.

Reid, K. A., *Impact of Technology on learning effectiveness. AT&T CEDL Newsletter*, 1995.

Hawkins, J., "Technology and the Organisation of Schooling (Technology in Education)", *Communication of the ACM*, Vol. 36, May 1993.

Hudspeth, D. R., and R. G. Brey, *Instructional Telecommunications, Principles and Applications*, New York: Praeger, 1986.

Lochte, R.H., *Interactive Television and Instruction*, Englewood Cliffs, NJ: Educational Technology Publications, 1993.

Portway, P., and Lane, C., *Technical Guide to Teleconferencing and Distance Learning*. San Ramon, CA: Applied Business telecommunications, 1992.

Sharma P.B., "Revitalising Technical Education for the New Millennium", *University News*, February 7, 2000.

Stuart, R. and Thomas, J. C., "The Implications of Education in Cyberspace", *Multimedia Review*, 1991.

Velayo, R. S., "Supplementary Classroom Instruction via Computer Conferencing", *Educational Technology*, 1994.

Whitelock D. and Scanlon E., "Motivation, Media and Motion: Reviewing a Computer Supported Collaborative Learning Experience, In *Proceedings of the European Conference on Artificial Intelligence in Education*, P. Brna, a. Paiva and J. Self (eds)., Euro AIED, Lisbon, 1996.

Wilson, M. E. and Whitelock, D., "Piloting a New Approach: Making Use of New Technology to Present a Distance Learning Computer Science Course", *Association for learning Technology Journal*, 1996.